Instant Vortex Air Fryer Oven Cookbook for Two

1001-Day Perfectly Portioned Recipes for Your Instant Vortex Air Fryer Oven to Fry, Bake, Grill & Roast and More

Lus Rables

© Copyright 2021 Lus Rables - All Rights Reserved.

In no way is it legal to reproduce, duplicate, or transmit any part of this document by either electronic means or in printed format. Recording of this publication is strictly prohibited, and any storage of this material is not allowed unless with written permission from the publisher. All rights reserved.

The information provided herein is stated to be truthful and consistent, in that any liability, regarding inattention or otherwise, by any usage or abuse of any policies, processes, or directions contained within is the solitary and complete responsibility of the recipient reader. Under no circumstances will any legal liability or blame be held against the publisher for any reparation, damages, or monetary loss due to the information herein, either directly or indirectly.

Respective authors own all copyrights not held by the publisher.

Legal Notice:

This book is copyright protected. This is only for personal use. You cannot amend, distribute, sell, use, quote or paraphrase any part of the content within this book without the consent of the author or copyright owner. Legal action will be pursued if this is breached.

Disclaimer Notice:

Please note the information contained within this document is for educational and entertainment purposes only. Every attempt has been made to provide accurate, up-to-date and reliable, complete information. No warranties of any kind are expressed or implied. Readers acknowledge that the author is not engaging in the rendering of legal, financial, medical or professional advice.

By reading this document, the reader agrees that under no circumstances are we responsible for any losses, direct or indirect, which are incurred as a result of the use of information contained within this document, including, but not limited to, errors, omissions, or inaccuracies.

Table of Contents

Introduction 5
Chapter 1: Instant Vortex Air Fryer Oven Basics 6
    Instant Vortex Air Fryer Oven 6
    How Instant Vortex Air Fryer Oven Works? 6
    Buttons and Functions of Instant Vortex Air Fryer Oven 7
    Benefits of Vortex Air Fryer Oven 8
Chapter 2: Breakfast & Brunch Recipes 10
    Almond Pumpkin Muffins 10
    Blueberry Breakfast Muffins 11
    Easy Egg Muffins 12
    Spinach Egg Muffins 13
    Broccoli Cheese Frittata 14
    Cheesy Egg Bites 15
    Delicious Breakfast Casserole 16
    Tomato Spinach Pepper Egg Cups . 17
    Sausage Omelet 18
    Chili Olive Breakfast Casserole 19
    Spicy Bacon Jalapeno Egg Cups 20
    Squash Casserole 21
Chapter 3: Poultry Recipes 22
    Curried Chicken Thighs 22
    Juicy & Crispy Chicken Drumsticks 23
    Baked Chicken Thighs 24
    Feta Turkey Patties 25
    Spicy Chicken Breasts 26
    Delicious Turkey Cutlets 27
    Tasty Jerk Chicken Wings 28
    Dijon Chicken Breasts 29
    Ranch Chicken with Broccoli 30
    Spinach Turkey Meatballs 31
    Tasty Chicken Nuggets 32
    Herb Chicken Breast 33
Chapter 4: Meat Recipes 34
    Flavorful Bone-in Pork Chops 34
    Cajun Pork Chops 35
    Flavorful Baked Pork Chops 36
    Meatballs 37
    Meatballs 38
    Steak Tips with Mushrooms 39
    Meatballs 40
    Delicious Steak Kebab 41
    Creole Cheese Pork Chops 42
    Tasty Stuffed Peppers 43
    Flavorful Beef Fajitas 44
    Delicious Beef Satay 45
Chapter 5: Vegetable Recipes 46
    Roasted Carrots Slices 46
    Healthy Cauliflower Roast 47
    Baked Cherry Tomatoes & Zucchini 48
    Zucchini Gratin 49
    Broccoli Coconut Loaf 50
    Flavorful Baked Okra 51
    Tasty Baked Cabbage 52
    Healthy Eggplant Salad 53
    Lemon Parmesan Broccoli 54
    Spinach Stuffed Peppers 55
    Cauliflower Rice 56
    Roasted Radishes 57
Chapter 6: Snacks & Appetizers 58
    Healthy Zucchini Chips 58
    Tuna Muffins 59
    Delicious Broccoli Tots 60
    Baked Eggplant Chips 61
    Meatballs 62
    Garlicky Mushrooms 63
    Salsa Jalapeno Poppers 64
    Savory Jalapeno Poppers 65
    Tasty Cauliflower Tots 66
    Ranch Chicken Wings 67
    Broccoli Cheese Balls 68
    Meatballs 69
Chapter 7: Seafood Recipes 70
    Delicious Baked Cod 70
    Greek Shrimp 71
    Easy Salmon Patties 72
    Chili Prawns 73

Delicious Baked Tilapia 74	Shrimp with Cherry Tomatoes 78
Baked Catfish................................ 75	Curried Cod Fillets 79
Dill Salmon Patties 76	Ginger Garlic Fish Fillet 80
Chipotle Shrimp 77	Lemon Garlic Cod 81

Chapter 8: Desserts Recipes **82**

Fudgey Flourless Chocolate Cake... 82	Zucchini Chocolate Bread 88
Coffee Cookies................................ 83	Healthy Chia Muffins 89
Zesty Lemon Muffins 84	Chocolate Macaroon....................... 90
Chocolate Chip Muffins.................. 85	Pumpkin Pie................................... 91
Cranberry Bread Loaf 86	Choco Chip Peanut Butter Muffins 92
Banana Almond Butter Bread 87	Pumpkin Butter Cookies 93

Chapter 9: Dehydrated Recipes **94**

Simple Tofu Jerky 94	Healthy Beet Chips 100
Parmesan Zucchini Chips 95	Marinated Eggplant Slices............. 101
Delicious BBQ Zucchini Chips 96	Lamb Jerky.................................... 102
Dehydrated Sweet Peppers.............. 97	Easy Kale Chips............................ 103
Crisp Green Bean Chips 98	Eggplant Chips 104
Dehydrated Bell Peppers................. 99	Turkey Jerky 105

Conclusion **106**

Introduction

If you are looking for an oven that will allow you to cook your meals at home within a short period without compromising your health, then the Instant Vortex Air Fryer Oven is the best choice. The Instant Vortex Air Fryer Oven makes cooking healthier by eliminating high fats, trans fats, sodium, and cholesterol from your favorite foods. This appliance can be used to cook any type of food you want, It's also a super healthy one because you will use up to 95% less oil so that you and your family can eat well, without giving up on evenly cooked, crispy, and delicious meals. Cooking healthy food is now much easier than ever!

In this cookbook you can find mouth-watering recipes that are very easy to produce, along with comprehensive instructions on how to start using your Instant Vortex Air Fryer Oven. Just get your Instant Vortex Air Fryer Oven ready and let my cookbook lead you through the simple steps needed to cook each meal. Nutritional information is included in all recipes, making it ideal to plan how many servings you want to prepare. Even if you are following a diet or just want to keep your daily calorie intake in check, the in-depth nutritional information would be useful.

This Instant Vortex Air Fryer Oven Cookbook for Two will increase your cooking desire for a crunchy and crispy experience in no time!

Chapter 1: Instant Vortex Air Fryer Oven Basics

Instant Vortex Air Fryer Oven

The instant vortex air fryer oven is one of the most advanced multi cooking appliances available in the market now. The biggest advantage of the vortex air fryer oven is that its large 10-quart capacity. It is capable to cook a large number of foods at once. Instant vortex air fryer oven is 7-in-1 multipurpose smart cooking appliances run on advanced microprocessor technology. It not only saves your kitchen space but also performs various cooking tasks into a single appliance. The smart programs are preset and design to get a perfect cooking result every time. Using these programs, you can easily air-fry crispy French fries, bake your favorite cakes and cookies, roast whole chicken at a time, broil fish or meat, reheat your leftover food and also dehydrate your favorite veggies and fruit slices. It is one of the best replacement options for your microwave, oven, dehydrator, and toaster.

The instant vortex air fryer oven comes with a user-friendly control system easily operates by anyone. No special skill requires operating your vortex air fryer oven. Just follow the instruction manual and cook healthy and delicious dishes at home. It cooks your food by circulating very hot air into the cooking chamber with the help of a convection fan. This will give you faster and even cooking results. It deep-fries your food into very less oil without compromising the taste and texture of deep-fried food. This will help to reduce your daily calorie consumption and make healthier and tasty dishes easily.

How Instant Vortex Air Fryer Oven Works?

The instant vortex air fryer requires 1500-watt energy and it is capable to produce a high temperature of 400° F. It works similarly as the convection oven technology. It uses hot air circulation technology in which very hot dry heats are circulating with the help of a convection fan around the food basket to cook your food fast and evenly from all the sides.

The instant vortex air fryer comes with 6 different accessories which help to make your daily cooking process easy. These accessories are 2 no's of Cooking Tray, Drip Pan, Rotisserie Basket, Rotisserie split with settings screw, 2 no's of rotisserie fork, and rotisserie lift. Before starting the actual cooking, process makes sure your instant vortex air fryer is kept on a flat surface.

- If preheat is require then preheat your vortex air fryer oven before placing the food inside. It takes approximately 3 to 4 minutes to preheat the air fryer oven.
- When the oven reaches the target temperature then the display indicates **Add Food**. Use hand protection gloves while placing your food into the cooking tray carefully and close the door.
- As per recipe requirements if the display indicates **turn Food** then turn, flip and shake the food.
- After finishing the cooking process display indicates **End** which means that the current running smart program has ended.

Buttons and Functions of Instant Vortex Air Fryer Oven

The vortex air fryer oven has various smart functions and buttons which makes your daily cooking simple and easy.

Touch Panel Display

The instant vortex air fryer oven comes with a big touch panel display. The display panel is equipped with automatic smart function and manual settings. The display helps to know the currently running programs, cooking time, cooking temperature, remainders, and error messages. When the air fryer oven is on standby mode then the display reads *OFF*.

Smart Functions

The vortex air fryer oven has equipped with smart functions, these functions are loaded with preset settings. While using these smart functions you never worry about time and temperature settings.

- **Air Fry:** Using this function you can air fry your favorite fried food into very less oil. A bowl of French fries requires just a tablespoon of oil to fry into an air fryer oven. It makes your French fries crispy from outside and tender from inside.
- **Roast:** Using rotisserie accessories you can roast your favorite meat, chicken, and beef under this function. Due to the 10-quart size, you can easily roast a whole chicken at a time.
- **Broil:** This function works similarly as grilling it helps to brown or toasting your food under direct radiant heat.
- **Bake:** This function is used to bake your favorite cakes, cookies, and desserts.

- **Reheat:** Using this function you can reheat pastries, frozen, and leftover food again.
- **Dehydrate:** This function allows you to dehydrate lots of food at once. It allows you to dehydrate your favorite fruits, vegetables, and meat slices.

Temp (+/-)

This function is used to adjust the temperature setting manually as per your recipe needs by pressing (+/-).

Time (+/-)

This function is used to adjust the time setting manually as per your recipe needs by processing (+/-).

Rotate

Once the cooking process is running you can use the rotate function to on and off the rotation of the rotisserie. This function is used while roasting your food.

Light

Using this function, you can see your food while cooking. Touching this function will ON and OFF the oven light. The light is automatically off after 2 minutes.

Cancel

Using this button, you can stop the current running program. While pressing this button the display reads OFF and the oven automatically goes into standby mode.

Start

This button is used to start the actual cooking process.

Benefits of Vortex Air Fryer Oven

The instant vortex air fryer has magical multi-cooking appliances that come with various benefits. These benefits include

1. **Requires less oil to cook your food**

   Compare to the traditional deep-frying method vortex air fryer requires very little oil to fry your food. It requires 85 % less oil compared with another deep-frying method. It fries your French fries within a tablespoon of oil without changing the taste and texture like deep-fried food. It makes your French fries crisp from outside and tender from inside.

2. **Saves cooking time**

Instant vortex air fryer oven is cooking your food by circulating very hot air into the cooking chamber. It blows 400° F hot air to cook your food very fast and it helps to save you cooking time. If you are one of the people who have a busy schedule, then the vortex air fryer oven is the best kitchen gadget for you. It cooks food faster and gives even cooking results within very less time.

3. **Multi-cooking appliance**

Vortex air fryer is one of the multi cooking appliances and the best replacement for microwave, oven, toaster, and dehydrator. It performs the task of the different appliances into a single cooking appliance. Due to this it not only saves your kitchen countertop space but also saves your money.

4. **Smart cooking programs**

Instant vortex air fryer loaded with smart cooking functions. It includes Air fry, Roast, Dehydrate, Reheat, Bake, and Broil. All these functions are pre-programmed, and you can use these functions without worrying about time and temperature settings.

5. **Safe appliance to use**

The vortex air fryer oven has come with a built-in protection feature against overheating. If the oven temperature exceeds over 450° F then the appliance is automatically shut off and the display reads error message E2.

Chapter 2: Breakfast & Brunch Recipes

Almond Pumpkin Muffins

Preparation Time: 10 minutes
Cooking Time: 25 minutes
Serve: 2

Ingredients:

- 4 eggs
- 1 tsp vanilla
- 1/2 cup pumpkin puree
- 1 tbsp pumpkin pie spice
- 1 tbsp baking powder
- 2/3 cup erythritol
- 1/3 cup coconut oil, melted
- 1 cup almond flour
- 1/2 tsp sea salt

Directions:

1. In a large bowl, mix together pumpkin pie spice, baking powder, erythritol, almond flour, and sea salt.
2. Stir in eggs, vanilla, coconut oil, and pumpkin puree until well combined.
3. Pour egg mixture into the 8 silicone muffin molds.
4. Select BAKE mode, then set the temperature to 350 F and the time to 25 minutes, then press start.
5. When the display shows Add Food then place muffin molds on the cooking tray and place in the vortex plus air fryer oven.
6. Serve and enjoy.

Nutritional Value (Amount per Serving):

- Calories 201
- Fat 18.4 g
- Carbohydrates 5.8 g
- Sugar 1.3 g
- Protein 6 g
- Cholesterol 82 mg

Blueberry Breakfast Muffins

Preparation Time: 10 minutes

Cooking Time: 25 minutes

Serve: 2

Ingredients:

- 2 eggs
- 1/2 cup fresh blueberries
- 1 tsp baking powder
- 6 drops stevia
- 1/4 cup butter, melted
- 1 cup heavy cream
- 2 cups almond flour
- 1/4 tsp lemon zest
- 1/2 tsp lemon extract

Directions:

1. In a mixing bowl, whisk eggs. Add remaining ingredients and mix until well combined.
2. Pour egg mixture into the 12 silicone muffin molds.
3. Select BAKE mode, then set the temperature to 350 F and the time to 25 minutes, then press start.
4. When the display shows Add Food then place muffin molds on the cooking tray and place in the vortex plus air fryer oven.
5. Serve and enjoy.

Nutritional Value (Amount per Serving):

- Calories 190
- Fat 17.6 g
- Carbohydrates 5.4 g
- Sugar 1.4 g
- Protein 5.2 g
- Cholesterol 51 mg

Easy Egg Muffins

Preparation Time: 10 minutes
Cooking Time: 30 minutes
Serve: 2

Ingredients:

- 6 eggs
- 1 red bell pepper, chopped
- 1 1/2 tsp dried oregano
- 1/3 cup unsweetened almond milk
- 1 tomato, chopped
- 1/2 cup feta cheese, crumbled
- 1/4 tsp pepper
- 1/8 tsp salt

Directions:

1. In a bowl, whisk eggs with milk, oregano, pepper, and salt.
2. Divide cheese, tomato, and bell pepper evenly in 12 silicone muffin molds.
3. Pour egg mixture over cheese vegetable mixture.
4. Select BAKE mode, then set the temperature to 350 F and the time to 25-30 minutes, then press start.
5. When the display shows Add Food then place muffin molds on the cooking tray and place in the vortex plus air fryer oven.
6. Serve and enjoy.

Nutritional Value (Amount per Serving):

- Calories 54
- Fat 3.7 g
- Carbohydrates 1.6 g
- Sugar 1.1 g
- Protein 3.9 g
- Cholesterol 87 mg

Spinach Egg Muffins

Preparation Time: 10 minutes

Cooking Time: 12 minutes

Serve: 2

Ingredients:

- 4 eggs
- 6 tbsp cheddar cheese, shredded
- 2 tbsp heavy cream
- 1/4 cup fresh baby spinach, chopped
- 4 bacon slices, cooked chopped
- Pepper
- Salt

Directions:

1. Divide spinach and bacon evenly into the 6 silicone muffin molds.
2. In a bowl, whisk eggs with cheddar cheese, heavy cream, pepper, and salt.
3. Pour egg mixture over spinach and bacon.
4. Select BAKE mode, then set the temperature to 380 F and the time to 12 minutes, then press start.
5. When the display shows Add Food then place silicone muffin molds on the cooking tray and place in the vortex plus air fryer oven.
6. Serve and enjoy.

Nutritional Value (Amount per Serving):

- Calories 157
- Fat 12.4 g
- Carbohydrates 0.7 g
- Sugar 0.3 g
- Protein 10.3 g
- Cholesterol 137 mg

Broccoli Cheese Frittata

Preparation Time: 10 minutes

Cooking Time: 25 minutes

Serve: 2

Ingredients:

- 10 eggs
- 2 cups broccoli, chopped
- 1/2 red bell pepper, diced
- 2 oz feta cheese, crumbled
- 2 tbsp olive oil
- 1 tsp black pepper
- 1 tsp salt

Directions:

1. In a bowl, whisk eggs with oil, pepper, and salt. Stir in broccoli, bell pepper, and feta cheese.
2. Pour egg mixture into the greased baking dish.
3. Select BAKE mode, then set the temperature to 400 F and the time to 25-30 minutes, then press start.
4. When the display shows Add Food then place the baking dish in the vortex plus air fryer oven.
5. Serve and enjoy.

Nutritional Value (Amount per Serving):

- Calories 276
- Fat 5.9 g
- Carbohydrates 5.9 g
- Sugar 3 g
- Protein 17.3 g
- Cholesterol 422 mg

Cheesy Egg Bites

Preparation Time: 10 minutes

Cooking Time: 20 minutes

Serve: 2

Ingredients:

- 3 eggs, lightly beaten
- 1 1/2 cups cheddar cheese
- 1/2 tsp baking powder
- 1/3 cup coconut flour
- 4 oz cream cheese, softened
- 2 cups ham, chopped
- 1/2 tsp garlic powder
- Pepper
- Salt

Directions:

1. Add all ingredients into the mixing bowl and mix until well combined then place in the refrigerator for 10-15 minutes.
2. Drop mixture onto the parchment-lined cooking tray using a cookie scoop.
3. Select BAKE mode, then set the temperature to 350 F and the time to 20 minutes, then press start.
4. When the display shows Add Food then place the cooking tray and place in the vortex plus air fryer oven.
5. Serve and enjoy.

Nutritional Value (Amount per Serving):

- Calories 434
- Fat 33.2 g
- Carbohydrates 5.4 g
- Sugar 0.7 g
- Protein 28.3 g
- Cholesterol 237 mg

Delicious Breakfast Casserole

Preparation Time: 10 minutes

Cooking Time: 35 minutes

Serve: 2

Ingredients:

- 2 eggs
- 4 egg whites
- 2/3 cup parmesan cheese, grated
- 2/3 cup chicken broth
- 1 lb Italian sausage
- 1/4 cup roasted red pepper, sliced
- 1/4 cup pesto sauce
- 1/8 tsp black pepper
- 1/4 tsp sea salt

Directions:

1. Brown sausage in a pan over medium heat.
2. Transfer sausage in greased baking dish.
3. Whisk remaining ingredients in a mixing bowl and pour over sausage.
4. Select BAKE mode, then set the temperature to 400 F and the time to 35 minutes, then press start.
5. When the display shows Add Food then place the baking dish in the vortex plus air fryer oven.
6. Serve and enjoy.

Nutritional Value (Amount per Serving):

- Calories 558
- Fat 44.3 g
- Carbohydrates 2.8 g
- Sugar 2 g
- Protein 35.6 g
- Cholesterol 191 mg

Tomato Spinach Pepper Egg Cups

Preparation Time: 10 minutes

Cooking Time: 20 minutes

Serve: 2

Ingredients:

- 12 eggs
- 1 cup fresh spinach, chopped
- 1/2 cup red bell pepper, chopped
- 1/2 cup tomatoes, chopped
- 4 tbsp water
- 1 tsp Italian seasoning
- 1/2 tsp pepper
- 1/4 tsp salt

Directions:

1. In a bowl, whisk eggs with water, Italian seasoning, pepper, and salt. Stir in spinach, bell pepper, and tomatoes.
2. Pour egg mixture into the 12 silicone muffin molds.
3. Select BAKE mode, then set the temperature to 350 F and the time to 20 minutes, then press start.
4. When the display shows Add Food then place muffin molds on the cooking tray and place in the vortex plus air fryer oven.
5. Serve and enjoy.

Nutritional Value (Amount per Serving):

- Calories 68
- Fat 4.5 g
- Carbohydrates 1.2 g
- Sugar 0.8 g
- Protein 5.7 g
- Cholesterol 164 mg

Sausage Omelet

Preparation Time: 10 minutes
Cooking Time: 25 minutes
Serve: 2

Ingredients:

- 7 eggs
- 1 lb breakfast sausage
- 1 tsp mustard
- 2 cups cheddar cheese, shredded
- 3/4 cup heavy cream
- 1/4 onion, chopped
- 1/2 bell pepper, chopped
- 1/4 tsp pepper
- 1/2 tsp salt

Directions:

1. Brown the sausage in a pan until brown. Add bell pepper and onion and cook for 2 minutes more.
2. Transfer sausage mixture into the baking dish.
3. In a bowl, whisk eggs with mustard, 1 3/4 cup cheese, heavy cream, pepper, and salt.
4. Pour egg mixture over sausage mixture. Sprinkle remaining cheese on top.
5. Select BAKE mode, then set the temperature to 350 F and the time to 20 minutes, then press start.
6. When the display shows Add Food then place the baking dish in the vortex plus air fryer oven.
7. Serve and enjoy.

Nutritional Value (Amount per Serving):

- Calories 271
- Fat 22.4 g
- Carbohydrates 1.4 g
- Sugar 0.7 g
- Protein 15.6 g
- Cholesterol 157 mg

Chili Olive Breakfast Casserole

Preparation Time: 10 minutes

Cooking Time: 35 minutes

Serve: 2

Ingredients:

- 12 eggs
- 4 oz green chilies, diced
- 2 cups cheddar cheese, grated
- 2 cups cottage cheese, rinsed and drained
- 6 oz olives, pitted and sliced
- 1/4 cup green onions, sliced
- Pepper
- Salt

Directions:

1. Add cottage cheese, cheddar cheese, green chilies, green onion, and olives in the greased baking dish.
2. Whisk beaten eggs and pour over cheese mixture. Season with pepper and salt.
3. Select BAKE mode, then set the temperature to 375 F and the time to 35 minutes, then press start.
4. When the display shows Add Food then place the baking dish in the vortex plus air fryer oven.
5. Serve and enjoy.

Nutritional Value (Amount per Serving):

- Calories 232
- Fat 13.1 g
- Carbohydrates 14.4 g
- Sugar 6.1 g
- Protein 16.2 g
- Cholesterol 40 mg

Spicy Bacon Jalapeno Egg Cups

Preparation Time: 10 minutes

Cooking Time: 20 minutes

Serve: 2

Ingredients:

- 9 eggs
- 1 1/2 jalapeno pepper, sliced
- 8 oz cheddar cheese, shredded
- 4 bacon slices, cooked and chopped
- 3/4 cup heavy cream
- Pepper
- Salt

Directions:

1. In a large bowl, whisk eggs with cheese, heavy cream, pepper, and salt.
2. Divide bacon and jalapeno pepper evenly in 12 silicone muffin molds.
3. Pour egg mixture into the prepared muffin molds.
4. Select BAKE mode, then set the temperature to 350 F and the time to 20 minutes, then press start.
5. When the display shows Add Food then place muffin molds on the cooking tray and place in the vortex plus air fryer oven.
6. Serve and enjoy.

Nutritional Value (Amount per Serving):

- Calories 184
- Fat 15 g
- Carbohydrates 0.9 g
- Sugar 0.4 g
- Protein 11.4 g
- Cholesterol 160 mg

Squash Casserole

Preparation Time: 10 minutes

Cooking Time: 25 minutes

Serve: 2

Ingredients:

- 12 eggs
- 2 cups spaghetti squash, cooked
- 1 cup cheddar cheese, shredded
- 1 cup heavy cream
- 4 tbsp butter, melted
- 1/2 cup bell pepper, diced
- Pepper
- Salt

Directions:

1. In a large bowl, add all ingredients and mix well until combine.
2. Pour mixture into the greased baking dish.
3. Select BAKE mode, then set the temperature to 350 F and the time to 25 minutes, then press start.
4. When the display shows Add Food then place the baking dish in the vortex plus air fryer oven.
5. Serve and enjoy.

Nutritional Value (Amount per Serving):

- Calories 352
- Fat 30.3 g
- Carbohydrates 4.6 g
- Sugar 1.3 g
- Protein 16.6 g
- Cholesterol 395 mg

Chapter 3: Poultry Recipes

Curried Chicken Thighs

Preparation Time: 10 minutes
Cooking Time: 20 minutes
Serve: 2

Ingredients:

- 1 lb chicken thighs, boneless and skinless
- 1/2 cup coconut milk
- 2 tbsp curry paste
- 2 tsp ginger, minced
- 1 tbsp garlic, chopped

Directions:

1. Add all ingredients into the zip-lock bag, seal bag, and shake well and place it in the refrigerator overnight.
2. Add marinated chicken with sauce in baking dish.
3. Select AIRFRY mode, then set the temperature to 180 F and the time to 20 minutes, then press start.
4. When the display shows Add Food then place the baking dish in the vortex plus air fryer oven.
5. Serve and enjoy.

Nutritional Value (Amount per Serving):

- Calories 341
- Fat 20 g
- Carbohydrates 5.1 g
- Sugar 1.1 g
- Protein 34.1 g
- Cholesterol 101 mg

Juicy & Crispy Chicken Drumsticks

Preparation Time: 10 minutes

Cooking Time: 45 minutes

Serve: 2

Ingredients:

- 2 lbs chicken drumsticks
- 1 tsp parsley, chopped
- 1 tsp onion powder
- 1 tsp garlic powder
- 1 tsp paprika
- 2 tbsp olive oil
- 1/2 tsp pepper
- 1/2 tsp salt

Directions:

1. Add chicken drumsticks and remaining ingredients into the zip-lock bag, seal bag and shake well to coat.
2. Arrange chicken drumsticks onto the cooking tray.
3. Select BAKE mode, then set the temperature to 400 F and the time to 40-45 minutes, then press start.
4. When the display shows Add Food then place the cooking tray in the vortex plus air fryer oven.
5. Serve and enjoy.

Nutritional Value (Amount per Serving):

- Calories 300
- Fat 13.4 g
- Carbohydrates 1 g
- Sugar 0.3 g
- Protein 41.8 g
- Cholesterol 133 mg

Baked Chicken Thighs

Preparation Time: 10 minutes
Cooking Time: 30 minutes
Serve: 2

Ingredients:

- 4 chicken thighs, pat dry with a paper towel
- 1 tsp dried parsley
- 1 tsp onion powder
- 1 tsp garlic powder
- Pepper
- Salt

Directions:

1. Mix together garlic powder, onion powder, dried parsley, pepper, and salt and rub all over chicken thighs.
2. Place chicken thighs onto the cooking tray.
3. Select BAKE mode, then set the temperature to 400 F and the time to 30 minutes, then press start.
4. When the display shows Add Food then place the cooking tray in the vortex plus air fryer oven.
5. Serve and enjoy.

Nutritional Value (Amount per Serving):

- Calories 282
- Fat 10.8 g
- Carbohydrates 1 g
- Sugar 0.4 g
- Protein 42.4 g
- Cholesterol 130 mg

Feta Turkey Patties

Preparation Time: 10 minutes

Cooking Time: 22 minutes

Serve: 2

Ingredients:

- 1 lb ground turkey
- 4 oz feta cheese, crumbled
- 1 1/4 cup spinach, chopped
- 1 tsp Italian seasoning
- 1 tbsp olive oil
- 1 tbsp garlic paste
- Pepper
- Salt

Directions:

1. Add all ingredients into the bowl and mix until well combined.
2. Make four equal shapes of patties from the mixture and place them onto the cooking tray.
3. Select AIRFRY mode, then set the temperature to 390 F and the time to 22 minutes, then press start.
4. When the display shows Add Food then place the cooking tray in the vortex plus air fryer oven.
5. Turn chicken patties through.
6. Serve and enjoy.

Nutritional Value (Amount per Serving):

- Calories 335
- Fat 22.4 g
- Carbohydrates 2.3 g
- Sugar 1.3 g
- Protein 35.5 g
- Cholesterol 142 mg

Spicy Chicken Breasts

Preparation Time: 10 minutes
Cooking Time: 45 minutes
Serve: 2

Ingredients:

- 4 chicken breasts
- 1 tbsp olive oil
- 2 tbsp Creole seasoning

Directions:

1. Brush chicken with oil and rub with Creole seasoning and place onto the cooking tray.
2. Select BAKE mode, then set the temperature to 400 F and the time to 40-45 minutes, then press start.
3. When the display shows Add Food then place the cooking tray in the vortex plus air fryer oven.
4. Serve and enjoy.

Nutritional Value (Amount per Serving):

- Calories 307
- Fat 14.3 g
- Carbohydrates 0 g
- Sugar 0 g
- Protein 42.2 g
- Cholesterol 130 mg

Delicious Turkey Cutlets

Preparation Time: 10 minutes

Cooking Time: 25 minutes

Serve: 2

Ingredients:

- 1 egg
- 1 1/2 lbs turkey cutlets
- 1/2 tsp garlic powder
- 1/2 tsp onion powder
- 1/2 tsp dried parsley
- 1/4 cup parmesan cheese, grated
- 1/2 cup almond flour
- Pepper
- Salt

Directions:

1. Season turkey cutlets with pepper and salt.
2. Add eggs into the small bowl and whisk well.
3. In a shallow dish, mix together parmesan cheese, garlic powder, onion powder, parsley, and almond flour.
4. Dip each turkey cutlet into the egg then coat with parmesan cheese mixture.
5. Place coated turkey cutlets onto the parchment-lined cooking tray.
6. Select BAKE mode, then set the temperature to 350 F and the time to 25 minutes, then press start.
7. When the display shows Add Food then place the cooking tray in the vortex plus air fryer oven.
8. Turn cutlet halfway through.
9. Serve and enjoy.

Nutritional Value (Amount per Serving):

- Calories 405
- Fat 17.8 g
- Carbohydrates 3.8 g
- Sugar 0.8 g
- Protein 56.1 g
- Cholesterol 174 mg

Tasty Jerk Chicken Wings

Preparation Time: 10 minutes
Cooking Time: 20 minutes
Serve: 2

Ingredients:

- 1 lb chicken wings
- 1 tsp olive oil
- 1 tbsp arrowroot
- 1 tbsp jerk seasoning
- Pepper
- Salt

Directions:

1. Add chicken wings and remaining ingredients into the mixing bowl and toss well.
2. Arrange chicken wings onto the cooking tray.
3. Select AIRFRY mode, then set the temperature to 380 F and the time to 20 minutes, then press start.
4. When the display shows Add Food then place the cooking tray in the vortex plus air fryer oven.
5. Turn chicken wings halfway through.
6. Serve and enjoy.

Nutritional Value (Amount per Serving):

- Calories 453
- Fat 19.2 g
- Carbohydrates 0.5 g
- Sugar 0 g
- Protein 65.8 g
- Cholesterol 202 mg

Dijon Chicken Breasts

Preparation Time: 10 minutes

Cooking Time: 15 minutes

Serve: 2

Ingredients:

- 1 1/2 lbs chicken breasts, boneless
- 1 tbsp fresh lemon juice
- 1 tbsp Dijon mustard
- 1/2 cup mayonnaise
- 1/4 tsp cayenne
- 1 tsp Italian seasoning
- 1 tbsp coconut aminos
- 1/2 tsp pepper
- 1 tsp sea salt

Directions:

1. In a small bowl, mix together mayonnaise, Italian seasoning, cayenne, coconut amino, lemon juice, mustard, pepper, and salt.
2. Add chicken and mayonnaise mixture into the zip-lock bag, seal bag, and place in the refrigerator overnight.
3. Seal the ziplock bag and place it in the refrigerator overnight.
4. Add marinated chicken onto the cooking tray.
5. Select AIRFRY mode, then set the temperature to 400 F and the time to 15 minutes, then press start.
6. When the display shows Add Food then place the cooking tray in the vortex plus air fryer oven.
7. Turn chicken halfway through.
8. Serve and enjoy.

Nutritional Value (Amount per Serving):

- Calories 300
- Fat 15.3 g
- Carbohydrates 5.6 g
- Sugar 1.4 g
- Protein 33.2 g
- Cholesterol 107 mg

Ranch Chicken with Broccoli

Preparation Time: 10 minutes

Cooking Time: 30 minutes

Serve: 2

Ingredients:

- 4 chicken breasts, skinless and boneless
- 1/2 cup ranch dressing
- 5 bacon slices, cooked and chopped
- 2 cups broccoli florets, blanched and chopped
- 1/3 cup mozzarella cheese, shredded
- 1 cup cheddar cheese, shredded

Directions:

1. Add chicken and broccoli into the baking dish and top with remaining ingredients.
2. Select BAKE mode, then set the temperature to 375 F and the time to 30 minutes, then press start.
3. When the display shows Add Food then place the baking dish in the vortex plus air fryer oven.
4. Serve and enjoy.

Nutritional Value (Amount per Serving):

- Calories 551
- Fat 30.8 g
- Carbohydrates 5.4 g
- Sugar 1.7 g
- Protein 60.4 g
- Cholesterol 187 mg

Spinach Turkey Meatballs

Preparation Time: 10 minutes

Cooking Time: 25 minutes

Serve: 2

Ingredients:

- 1 egg
- 2 lbs ground turkey
- 1/2 tsp garlic, minced
- 1 small onion, minced
- 10 oz frozen spinach, thawed, drained & chopped
- 1/4 tsp pepper
- 1 1/2 tsp salt

Directions:

1. Add all ingredients into the bowl and mix until well combined.
2. Make small balls from meat mixture and place onto the parchment-lined cooking tray.
3. Select BAKE mode, then set the temperature to 400 F and the time to 25 minutes, then press start.
4. When the display shows Add Food then place the cooking tray in the vortex plus air fryer oven.
5. Serve and enjoy.

Nutritional Value (Amount per Serving):

- Calories 322
- Fat 17.5 g
- Carbohydrates 3 g
- Sugar 0.8 g
- Protein 43.8 g
- Cholesterol 181 mg

Tasty Chicken Nuggets

Preparation Time: 10 minutes

Cooking Time: 25 minutes

Serve: 2

Ingredients:

- 1 1/2 lbs chicken breast, boneless & cut into chunks
- 1/4 cup parmesan cheese, shredded
- 1/4 cup mayonnaise
- 1/2 tsp garlic powder
- 1/4 tsp salt

Directions:

1. In a bowl, mix together mayonnaise, garlic powder, cheese, and salt. Add chicken chunks and toss until well coated.
2. Arrange chicken chunks onto the parchment-lined cooking tray.
3. Select BAKE mode, then set the temperature to 400 F and the time to 25 minutes, then press start.
4. When the display shows Add Food then place the cooking tray in the vortex plus air fryer oven.
5. Serve and enjoy.

Nutritional Value (Amount per Serving):

- Calories 270
- Fat 10.4 g
- Carbohydrates 4 g
- Sugar 1 g
- Protein 38.1 g
- Cholesterol 117 mg

Herb Chicken Breast

Preparation Time: 10 minutes
Cooking Time: 25 minutes
Serve: 2

Ingredients:

- 4 chicken breasts, skinless & boneless
- 1 tbsp olive oil

For rub:

- 1 tsp oregano
- 1 tsp thyme
- 1 tsp parsley
- 1 tsp onion powder
- 1 tsp basil
- Pepper
- Salt

Directions:

1. In a small bowl mix together all rub ingredients.
2. Brush chicken with oil and rub with herb mixture.
3. Arrange chicken onto the cooking tray.
4. Select BAKE mode, then set the temperature to 390 F and the time to 25 minutes, then press start.
5. When the display shows Add Food then place the cooking tray in the vortex plus air fryer oven.
6. Turn chicken halfway through.
7. Serve and enjoy.

Nutritional Value (Amount per Serving):

- Calories 312
- Fat 14.4 g
- Carbohydrates 0.9 g
- Sugar 0.2 g
- Protein 42.4 g
- Cholesterol 130 mg

Chapter 4: Meat Recipes

Flavorful Bone-in Pork Chops

Preparation Time: 10 minutes
Cooking Time: 20 minutes
Serve: 2

Ingredients:

- 1 1/2 lb pork chops, bone-in
- 1 tsp paprika
- 1/2 tsp onion powder
- 1/2 tsp pepper
- 4 tbsp olive oil
- 1 tsp salt

Directions:

1. In a small bowl, mix together paprika, onion powder, pepper, and salt.
2. Brush pork chops with oil and rub with spice mixture.
3. Place pork chops onto the cooking tray.
4. Select BAKE mode, then set the temperature to 400 F and the time to 15-20 minutes, then press start.
5. When the display shows Add Food then place the cooking tray in the vortex plus air fryer oven.
6. Serve and enjoy.

Nutritional Value (Amount per Serving):

- Calories 890
- Fat 75.1 g
- Carbohydrates 0.9 g
- Sugar 0.2 g
- Protein 51.1 g
- Cholesterol 195 mg

Cajun Pork Chops

Preparation Time: 10 minutes
Cooking Time: 10 minutes
Serve: 2

Ingredients:
- 4 pork chops
- 2 tbsp olive oil
- 1 tbsp Cajun seasoning

Directions:
1. Brush pork chops with oil and season with Cajun seasoning.
2. Place pork chops onto the cooking tray.
3. Select AIRFRY mode, then set the temperature to 375 F and the time to 10 minutes, then press start.
4. When the display shows Add Food then place the cooking tray in the vortex plus air fryer oven.
5. Turn pork chops halfway through.
6. Serve and enjoy.

Nutritional Value (Amount per Serving):
- Calories 316
- Fat 26.9 g
- Carbohydrates 0 g
- Sugar 0 g
- Protein 18 g
- Cholesterol 69 mg

Flavorful Baked Pork Chops

Preparation Time: 10 minutes
Cooking Time: 18 minutes
Serve: 2

Ingredients:

- 4 pork chops, boneless
- 2 tbsp olive oil
- 1 tsp oregano
- 1 tsp onion powder
- 1 tsp garlic powder
- 1 tbsp paprika
- Pepper
- Salt

Directions:

1. Brush pork chops with 1 tablespoon of olive oil.
2. Mix together paprika, garlic powder, onion powder, oregano, pepper, and salt and rub all over pork chops.
3. Place pork chops onto the parchment-lined cooking tray. Drizzle remaining oil over pork chops.
4. Select BAKE mode, then set the temperature to 400 F and the time to 18 minutes, then press start.
5. When the display shows Add Food then place the cooking tray in the vortex plus air fryer oven.
6. Serve and enjoy.

Nutritional Value (Amount per Serving):

- Calories 327
- Fat 27.2 g
- Carbohydrates 2.2 g
- Sugar 0.6 g
- Protein 18.5 g
- Cholesterol 69 mg

Meatballs

Preparation Time: 10 minutes
Cooking Time: 20 minutes
Serve: 2

Ingredients:

- 1 lb ground beef
- 1/2 small onion, chopped
- 1 egg, lightly beaten
- 2 garlic cloves, minced
- 1 tbsp basil, chopped
- 1/4 cup parmesan cheese, grated
- 1 tbsp parsley, chopped
- 1 tbsp rosemary, chopped
- 2 tbsp coconut milk
- 1/2 cup almond flour
- Pepper
- Salt

Directions:

1. Add all ingredients into the bowl and mix until well combined.
2. Make small balls from meat mixture and place onto the parchment-lined cooking tray.
3. Select BAKE mode, then set the temperature to 375 F and the time to 20 minutes, then press start.
4. When the display shows Add Food then place the cooking tray in the vortex plus air fryer oven.
5. Serve and enjoy.

Nutritional Value (Amount per Serving):

- Calories 351
- Fat 18.3 g
- Carbohydrates 5.7 g
- Sugar 1.2 g
- Protein 41.1 g
- Cholesterol 146 mg

Meatballs

Preparation Time: 10 minutes
Cooking Time: 20 minutes
Serve: 2

Ingredients:

- 1/2 lb ground beef
- 1/2 lb Italian sausage
- 1/2 cup mozzarella cheese, shredded
- 1/2 tsp black pepper
- 1/2 tsp garlic powder
- 1/2 tsp onion powder
- Salt

Directions:

1. Add all ingredients into the large mixing bowl and mix until well combined.
2. Make meatballs from mixture and place onto the cooking tray.
3. Select AIRFRY mode, then set the temperature to 370 F and the time to 15-20 minutes, then press start.
4. When the display shows Add Food then place the cooking tray in the vortex plus air fryer oven.
5. Serve and enjoy.

Nutritional Value (Amount per Serving):

- Calories 310
- Fat 20.3 g
- Carbohydrates 0.8 g
- Sugar 0.2 g
- Protein 29.3 g
- Cholesterol 100 mg

Steak Tips with Mushrooms

Preparation Time: 10 minutes

Cooking Time: 10 minutes

Serve: 2

Ingredients:

- 1 lb ribeye steaks, cut into bite-size pieces
- 1 1/2 tbsp olive oil
- 2 tbsp Worcestershire sauce
- 8 oz mushrooms, sliced
- Pepper
- Salt

Directions:

1. Add steak pieces, oil, Worcestershire sauce, mushrooms, pepper, and salt into the mixing bowl and toss well.
2. Transfer steak and mushroom mixture onto the parchment-lined cooking tray.
3. Select AIRFRY mode, then set the temperature to 400 F and the time to 10 minutes, then press start.
4. When the display shows Add Food then place the cooking tray in the vortex plus air fryer oven.
5. Stir steak and mushrooms halfway through.
6. Serve and enjoy.

Nutritional Value (Amount per Serving):

- Calories 224
- Fat 16.4 g
- Carbohydrates 3.4 g
- Sugar 2.5 g
- Protein 1.8 g
- Cholesterol 0 mg

Meatballs

Preparation Time: 10 minutes
Cooking Time: 20 minutes
Serve: 2

Ingredients:

- 1 lb ground beef
- 2 tbsp fresh parsley, chopped
- 1/2 cup almond flour
- 1/4 cup onion, chopped
- 3 tbsp mushrooms, chopped
- 1/2 tsp pepper
- 1 tsp salt

Directions:

1. In a bowl, mix together ground beef, parsley, onions, and mushrooms.
2. Add remaining ingredients and mix until combined.
3. Make small balls from the mixture and place onto the cooking tray.
4. Select AIRFRY mode, then set the temperature to 350 F and the time to 20 minutes, then press start.
5. When the display shows Add Food then place the cooking tray in the vortex plus air fryer oven.
6. Serve and enjoy.

Nutritional Value (Amount per Serving):

- Calories 99
- Fat 4.7 g
- Carbohydrates 1.4 g
- Sugar 0.3 g
- Protein 12.6 g
- Cholesterol 34 mg

Delicious Steak Kebab

Preparation Time: 10 minutes

Cooking Time: 10 minutes

Serve: 2

Ingredients:

- 1 lb sirloin steak, cut into 1-inch pieces
- 1 red bell pepper, cut into 1-inch pieces
- 1 onion, cut into 1-inch pieces

For marinade:

- 2 tbsp vinegar
- 2 tbsp olive oil
- 1/4 cup soy sauce
- 1 tsp ginger garlic paste
- 1 tsp pepper

Directions:

1. Add meat and remaining ingredients into the zip-lock bag, seal bag and shake well and place in the refrigerator overnight.
2. Thread marinated steak pieces, bell pepper, and onion onto the skewers.
3. Place skewers onto the cooking tray.
4. Select AIRFRY mode, then set the temperature to 350 F and the time to 10 minutes, then press start.
5. When the display shows Add Food then place the cooking tray in the vortex plus air fryer oven.
6. Serve and enjoy.

Nutritional Value (Amount per Serving):

- Calories 309
- Fat 14.5 g
- Carbohydrates 7.2 g
- Sugar 3 g
- Protein 36.3 g
- Cholesterol 101 mg

Creole Cheese Pork Chops

Preparation Time: 10 minutes

Cooking Time: 12 minutes

Serve: 2

Ingredients:

- 1 1/2 lbs pork chops, boneless
- 1 tsp Creole seasoning
- 1/4 cup mozzarella cheese, grated
- 1/3 cup almond flour
- 1 tsp paprika
- 1 tsp garlic powder

Directions:

1. Add pork chops and remaining ingredients into the zip-lock bag, seal bag shakes well.
2. Place coated pork chops onto the parchment-lined cooking tray.
3. Select AIRFRY mode, then set the temperature to 360 F and the time to 12 minutes, then press start.
4. When the display shows Add Food then place the cooking tray in the vortex plus air fryer oven.
5. Serve and enjoy.

Nutritional Value (Amount per Serving):

- Calories 404
- Fat 31.6 g
- Carbohydrates 1.9 g
- Sugar 0.4 g
- Protein 27.3 g
- Cholesterol 98 mg

Tasty Stuffed Peppers

Preparation Time: 10 minutes

Cooking Time: 8 minutes

Serve: 2

Ingredients:

- 6 jalapeno peppers, cut in half & remove seeds
- 1 1/2 tbsp taco seasoning
- 1/2 lb ground pork
- 1/4 cup mozzarella cheese, shredded

Directions:

1. Browned the meat in a pan. Remove pan from heat.
2. Add taco seasoning and mix well.
3. Stuff meat into each jalapeno half.
4. Place stuffed jalapeno peppers onto the cooking tray and top with cheese.
5. Select AIRFRY mode, then set the temperature to 320 F and the time to 8 minutes, then press start.
6. When the display shows Add Food then place the cooking tray in the vortex plus air fryer oven.
7. Serve and enjoy.

Nutritional Value (Amount per Serving):

- Calories 34
- Fat 1 g
- Carbohydrates 0.7 g
- Sugar 0.2 g
- Protein 5.4 g
- Cholesterol 15 mg

Flavorful Beef Fajitas

Preparation Time: 10 minutes
Cooking Time: 8 minutes
Serve: 2

Ingredients:

- 1 lb beef flank steak, sliced
- 1/2 tbsp chili powder
- 3 tbsp olive oil
- 1/2 onion, sliced
- 1 green bell pepper, sliced
- 1 red bell pepper, sliced
- 1 tsp garlic powder
- 1 tsp paprika
- 1 1/2 tsp cumin
- Pepper
- Salt

Directions:

1. Add meat and remaining ingredients into the bowl and toss to coat.
2. Transfer beef mixture into the baking dish.
3. Select AIRFRY mode, then set the temperature to 390 F and the time to 5-8 minutes, then press start.
4. When the display shows Add Food then place the baking dish in the vortex plus air fryer oven.
5. Serve and enjoy.

Nutritional Value (Amount per Serving):

- Calories 326
- Fat 18.1 g
- Carbohydrates 2.4 g
- Sugar 2.4 g
- Protein 35.3 g
- Cholesterol 101 mg

Delicious Beef Satay

Preparation Time: 10 minutes

Cooking Time: 8 minutes

Serve: 2

Ingredients:

- 1 lb beef flank steak, sliced into long strips
- 1 tbsp fish sauce
- 2 tbsp olive oil
- 1 tsp hot sauce
- 1 tbsp Swerve
- 1 tbsp garlic, minced
- 1 tbsp ginger, minced
- 1 tbsp soy sauce
- 1/2 cup cilantro, chopped
- 1 tsp ground coriander

Directions:

1. Add all ingredients into the zip-lock bag, seal bag, and shake well. Place into the refrigerator for 1 hour.
2. Place marinated meat onto the cooking tray.
3. Select AIRFRY mode, then set the temperature to 400 F and the time to 8 minutes, then press start.
4. When the display shows Add Food then place the cooking tray in the vortex plus air fryer oven.
5. Serve and enjoy.

Nutritional Value (Amount per Serving):

- Calories 568
- Fat 28.3 g
- Carbohydrates 5.4 g
- Sugar 0.7 g
- Protein 70.4 g
- Cholesterol 203 mg

Chapter 5: Vegetable Recipes

Roasted Carrots Slices

Preparation Time: 10 minutes
Cooking Time: 14 minutes
Serve: 2

Ingredients:

- 6 carrots peel and slice into thick chips
- 1 tbsp fresh parsley, chopped
- 1 tbsp oregano
- 2 tbsp olive oil
- Pepper
- Salt

Directions:

1. Add carrots into the baking dish and drizzle with olive oil.
2. Select AIRFRY mode, then set the temperature to 360 F and the time to 12 minutes, then press start.
3. When the display shows Add Food then place the baking dish in the vortex plus air fryer oven.
4. Add oregano, pepper, and salt in a baking dish and stir well and AIRFRY for 2 minutes more.
5. Garnish with chopped parsley and serve.

Nutritional Value (Amount per Serving):

- Calories 81
- Fat 7.2 g
- Carbohydrates 4.8 g
- Sugar 2.1 g
- Protein 0.5 g
- Cholesterol 0 mg

Healthy Cauliflower Roast

Preparation Time: 10 minutes

Cooking Time: 25 minutes

Serve: 2

Ingredients:

- 1 medium cauliflower head, cut into florets
- 1/4 tsp garlic powder
- 1/2 tsp pepper
- 2 tbsp olive oil
- 1 tsp sea salt

Directions:

1. Add cauliflower florets and remaining ingredients into the mixing bowl and toss well.
2. Spread cauliflower florets onto the cooking tray.
3. Select BAKE mode, then set the temperature to 400 F and the time to 25-30 minutes, then press start.
4. When the display shows Add Food then place the cooking tray in the vortex plus air fryer oven.
5. Serve and enjoy.

Nutritional Value (Amount per Serving):

- Calories 97
- Fat 7.2 g
- Carbohydrates 7.9 g
- Sugar 3.5 g
- Protein 2.9 g
- Cholesterol 0 mg

Baked Cherry Tomatoes & Zucchini

Preparation Time: 10 minutes

Cooking Time: 35 minutes

Serve: 2

Ingredients:

- 2 1/2 lbs zucchini, cut into quarters
- 6 garlic cloves, crushed
- 10 oz cherry tomatoes cut in half
- 1/3 cup parsley, chopped
- 1 tsp dried basil
- 1/2 cup parmesan cheese, shredded
- 1/2 tsp black pepper
- 3/4 tsp salt

Directions:

1. Add all ingredients except parsley into the large mixing bowl and stir well to combine.
2. Pour egg mixture into the greased baking dish.
3. Select BAKE mode, then set the temperature to 350 F and the time to 35 minutes, then press start.
4. When the display shows Add Food then place the baking dish in the vortex plus air fryer oven.
5. Garnish with parsley and serve.

Nutritional Value (Amount per Serving):

- Calories 69
- Fat 2.1 g
- Carbohydrates 9.8 g
- Sugar 4.6 g
- Protein 5.4 g
- Cholesterol 5 mg

Zucchini Gratin

Preparation Time: 10 minutes

Cooking Time: 30 minutes

Serve: 2

Ingredients:

- 1 large egg, lightly beaten
- 1 1/4 cup unsweetened almond milk
- 3 medium zucchinis, sliced
- 1 tbsp Dijon mustard
- 1/2 cup nutritional yeast
- 1 tsp sea salt

Directions:

1. Arrange zucchini slices in the greased baking dish.
2. In a saucepan, heat almond milk over low heat and stir in Dijon mustard, nutritional yeast, and sea salt. Add beaten egg and whisk well.
3. Pour sauce over zucchini slices.
4. Select BAKE mode, then set the temperature to 400 F and the time to 25-30 minutes, then press start.
5. When the display shows Add Food then place the baking dish in the vortex plus air fryer oven.
6. Serve and enjoy.

Nutritional Value (Amount per Serving):

- Calories 124
- Fat 2.5 g
- Carbohydrates 11.2 g
- Sugar 1.7 g
- Protein 14.1 g
- Cholesterol 47 mg

Broccoli Coconut Loaf

Preparation Time: 10 minutes
Cooking Time: 30 minutes
Serve: 2

Ingredients:

- 5 eggs, lightly beaten
- 3/4 cup broccoli florets, chopped
- 1 cup cheddar cheese, shredded
- 2 tsp baking powder
- 3 1/1 tbsp coconut flour
- 1 tsp salt

Directions:

1. Add all ingredients into the bowl and mix well.
2. Pour egg mixture into the greased loaf pan.
3. Select BAKE mode, then set the temperature to 350 F and the time to 30 minutes, then press start.
4. When the display shows Add Food then place the loaf pan in the vortex plus air fryer oven.
5. Slice and serve.

Nutritional Value (Amount per Serving):

- Calories 209
- Fat 13.5 g
- Carbohydrates 8.9 g
- Sugar 1.5 g
- Protein 13.2 g
- Cholesterol 187 mg

Flavorful Baked Okra

Preparation Time: 10 minutes

Cooking Time: 15 minutes

Serve: 2

Ingredients:

- 1 lb fresh okra, cut into 1/2-inch pieces
- 1 tsp paprika
- 2 tbsp olive oil
- 1/8 tsp cayenne pepper
- Salt

Directions:

1. In a large bowl, add okra and remaining ingredients and toss well.
2. Spread okra onto the cooking tray.
3. Select BAKE mode, then set the temperature to 400 F and the time to 15 minutes, then press start.
4. When the display shows Add Food then place the cooking tray in the vortex plus air fryer oven.
5. Serve and enjoy.

Nutritional Value (Amount per Serving):

- Calories 107
- Fat 7.3 g
- Carbohydrates 8.8 g
- Sugar 1.7 g
- Protein 2.3 g
- Cholesterol 0 mg

Tasty Baked Cabbage

Preparation Time: 10 minutes

Cooking Time: 25 minutes

Serve: 2

Ingredients:

- 2 lbs medium cabbage, thin shreds
- 3 tbsp butter, melted
- 1 tbsp paprika
- 1 tbsp garlic powder
- 1 tsp salt

Directions:

1. Add cabbage, butter, paprika, garlic powder, and salt into the mixing bowl and toss well.
2. Add cabbage mixture into the baking dish.
3. Select BAKE mode, then set the temperature to 400 F and the time to 25 minutes, then press start.
4. When the display shows Add Food then place the baking dish in the vortex plus air fryer oven.
5. Serve and enjoy.

Nutritional Value (Amount per Serving):

- Calories 224
- Fat 17.8 g
- Carbohydrates 11.8 g
- Sugar 1.4 g
- Protein 3.7 g
- Cholesterol 46 mg

Healthy Eggplant Salad

Preparation Time: 10 minutes

Cooking Time: 25 minutes

Serve: 2

Ingredients:

- 1 lb eggplant, cut into slices
- 1/4 cup olive oil
- 1 tbsp fresh lemon juice
- 1 tbsp parsley, chopped
- 1 tbsp cilantro, chopped
- 1/2 tsp paprika
- 1 tsp ground cumin
- 1 garlic clove, grated
- 1/2 tsp salt

Directions:

1. Brush eggplant slices with 2 tbsp oil.
2. Place eggplant slices onto a cooking tray.
3. Select BAKE mode, then set the temperature to 400 F and the time to 25 minutes, then press start.
4. When the display shows Add Food then place the cooking tray in the vortex plus air fryer oven.
5. In a bowl, mix together the remaining ingredients and pour over eggplant slices.
6. Mix well and serve.

Nutritional Value (Amount per Serving):

- Calories 94
- Fat 8.7 g
- Carbohydrates 5 g
- Sugar 2.4 g
- Protein 0.9 g
- Cholesterol 0 mg

Lemon Parmesan Broccoli

Preparation Time: 10 minutes
Cooking Time: 25 minutes
Serve: 2

Ingredients:

- 4 cups broccoli florets
- 4 garlic cloves, sliced
- 3 tbsp coconut oil
- 1 lemon juice
- 1 cup parmesan cheese, grated
- 1/2 tsp pepper
- 1 1/2 tsp salt

Directions:

1. In a bowl, toss broccoli florets with coconut oil. Add garlic and season with pepper and salt.
2. Spread broccoli in baking dish.
3. Select BAKE mode, then set the temperature to 400 F and the time to 20 minutes, then press start.
4. When the display shows Add Food then place the baking dish in the vortex plus air fryer oven.
5. Sprinkle with half parmesan cheese and BAKE for 5 minutes more.
6. Add remaining parmesan cheese and lemon juice. Stir well and serve.

Nutritional Value (Amount per Serving):

- Calories 356
- Fat 30.3 g
- Carbohydrates 8.4 g
- Sugar 1.6 g
- Protein 17.1 g
- Cholesterol 32 mg

Spinach Stuffed Peppers

Preparation Time: 10 minutes

Cooking Time: 45 minutes

Serve: 2

Ingredients:

- 4 eggs
- 2 bell peppers, sliced in half and remove seeds
- 1/2 cup parmesan cheese, grated
- 1/2 cup mozzarella cheese, shredded
- 1/2 cup ricotta cheese
- 1/4 cup baby spinach
- 1/4 tsp dried parsley
- 1 tsp garlic powder

Directions:

1. Add three cheeses, parsley, garlic powder, and eggs in food processor and process until combined.
2. Pour egg mixture into each pepper half and top with baby spinach.
3. Place stuffed peppers in a baking dish.
4. Select BAKE mode, then set the temperature to 375 F and the time to 35-45 minutes, then press start.
5. When the display shows Add Food then place the baking dish in the vortex plus air fryer oven.
6. Serve and enjoy.

Nutritional Value (Amount per Serving):

- Calories 156
- Fat 8.8 g
- Carbohydrates 7.4 g
- Sugar 3.6 g
- Protein 12.7 g
- Cholesterol 179 mg

Cauliflower Rice

Preparation Time: 10 minutes
Cooking Time: 15 minutes
Serve: 2

Ingredients:

- 1 cauliflower head, cut into florets
- 2 chilies, chopped
- 2 garlic cloves, chopped
- 1 tomato, chopped
- 1 onion, chopped
- 2 tbsp olive oil
- 1 tsp white pepper
- 1 tsp black pepper
- 1 tbsp dried thyme
- 2 tbsp tomato paste
- 1/2 tsp salt

Directions:

1. Add cauliflower florets into the food processor and process until it looks like rice.
2. Stir in tomato paste, tomatoes, and spices and mix well.
3. Spread cauliflower mixture in a baking dish and drizzle with olive oil.
4. Select BAKE mode, then set the temperature to 400 F and the time to 15 minutes, then press start.
5. When the display shows Add Food then place the baking dish in the vortex plus air fryer oven.
6. Serve and enjoy.

Nutritional Value (Amount per Serving):

- Calories 138
- Fat 9.7 g
- Carbohydrates 12.8 g
- Sugar 5.7 g
- Protein 3.1 g
- Cholesterol 0 mg

Roasted Radishes

Preparation Time: 10 minutes

Cooking Time: 30 minutes

Serve: 2

Ingredients:

- 3 cups radish, clean and halved
- 8 black peppercorns, crushed
- 3 tbsp olive oil
- 2 tbsp fresh rosemary, chopped
- 2 tsp sea salt

Directions:

1. Add radishes, salt, peppercorns, rosemary, and 2 tablespoons of olive oil in a bowl and toss well.
2. Pour radishes mixture onto the cooking tray.
3. Select BAKE mode, then set the temperature to 400 F and the time to 30 minutes, then press start.
4. When the display shows Add Food then place the cooking tray in the vortex plus air fryer oven.
5. Heat remaining olive oil in a pan over medium heat.
6. Add baked radishes in the pan and sauté for 2 minutes.
7. Serve and enjoy.

Nutritional Value (Amount per Serving):

- Calories 220
- Fat 21.7 g
- Carbohydrates 8.3 g
- Sugar 3.2 g
- Protein 1.4 g
- Cholesterol 0 mg

Chapter 6: Snacks & Appetizers

Healthy Zucchini Chips

Preparation Time: 10 minutes
Cooking Time: 15 minutes
Serve: 2

Ingredients:

- 2 medium zucchinis, sliced into rounds
- 3/4 tsp garlic powder
- 2/3 cup Asiago cheese, grated
- 4 tbsp olive oil
- 1/4 tsp smoked paprika
- Pepper
- salt

Directions:

1. In a bowl, toss zucchini with garlic powder, paprika, oil, pepper, and salt until well coated.
2. Arrange zucchini slices onto the cooking tray and sprinkle with grated cheese on top.
3. Select BAKE mode, then set the temperature to 375 F and the time to 15 minutes, then press start.
4. When the display shows Add Food then place the cooking tray in the vortex plus air fryer oven.
5. Serve and enjoy.

Nutritional Value (Amount per Serving):

- Calories 93
- Fat 8.8 g
- Carbohydrates 1.9 g
- Sugar 0.9 g
- Protein 2.6 g
- Cholesterol 1.9 mg

Tuna Muffins

Preparation Time: 10 minutes
Cooking Time: 25 minutes
Serve: 2

Ingredients:

- 2 large eggs
- 1 can tuna, flaked
- 1 tsp cayenne pepper
- 1 celery stalk, chopped
- 1 1/2 cups cheddar cheese, shredded
- 1/4 cup sour cream
- 1/4 cup mayonnaise
- Pepper
- Salt

Directions:

1. Add eggs and remaining ingredients into the mixing bowl and mix well.
2. Pour mixture into the 8 silicone muffin molds.
3. Select BAKE mode, then set the temperature to 350 F and the time to 25 minutes, then press start.
4. When the display shows Add Food then place silicone muffin molds on the cooking tray and place in the vortex plus air fryer oven.
5. Serve and enjoy.

Nutritional Value (Amount per Serving):

- Calories 190
- Fat 14.1 g
- Carbohydrates 2.6 g
- Sugar 0.7 g
- Protein 13.1 g
- Cholesterol 81 mg

Delicious Broccoli Tots

Preparation Time: 10 minutes

Cooking Time: 16 minutes

Serve: 2

Ingredients:

- 1 egg
- 2 tbsp almond flour
- 2 cups cheddar cheese, shredded
- 2 cups broccoli rice, cooked
- 1 tsp Italian seasoning
- Pepper
- Salt

Directions:

1. Add all ingredients into the mixing bowl and mix until well combined.
2. Make small balls from mixture and place on a cooking tray.
3. Place drip pan into the bottom of the vortex plus air fryer oven cooking chamber.
4. Select BAKE mode, then set the temperature to 400 F and the time to 16 minutes, then press start.
5. When the display shows Add Food then place the cooking tray in the vortex plus air fryer oven.
6. Turn broccoli tots halfway through.
7. Serve and enjoy.

Nutritional Value (Amount per Serving):

- Calories 322
- Fat 24.4 g
- Carbohydrates 8.2 g
- Sugar 1.1 g
- Protein 17.7 g
- Cholesterol 101 mg

Baked Eggplant Chips

Preparation Time: 5 minutes

Cooking Time: 20 minutes

Serve: 2

Ingredients:

- 1 eggplant, cut into 1-inch slices
- 1/2 tsp Italian seasoning
- 1 tsp paprika
- 2 tbsp olive oil
- 1/8 tsp cayenne
- 1/2 tsp red pepper
- 1 tsp garlic powder

Directions:

1. Add all ingredients into the mixing bowl and toss well.
2. Arrange eggplant slices onto the cooking tray.
3. Select AIRFRY mode, then set the temperature to 375 F and the time to 20 minutes, then press start.
4. When the display shows Add Food then place the cooking tray in the vortex plus air fryer oven.
5. Turn eggplant slices halfway through.
6. Serve and enjoy.

Nutritional Value (Amount per Serving):

- Calories 99
- Fat 7.5 g
- Carbohydrates 8.8 g
- Sugar 4.5 g
- Protein 1.5 g
- Cholesterol 0 mg

Meatballs

Preparation Time: 10 minutes
Cooking Time: 25 minutes
Serve: 2

Ingredients:

- 1 egg, lightly beaten
- 1 lb ground turkey
- 1 tsp garlic powder
- 1 1/2 tbsp olive oil
- 3/4 cup parmesan cheese, grated
- 1/4 cup fresh parsley, chopped
- 1/2 tsp cayenne
- 1 tsp paprika
- 1 tsp onion powder
- 1/2 tsp salt

Directions:

1. Add all ingredients into the mixing bowl and mix until well combined.
2. Make small balls from the meat mixture and place them onto the cooking tray.
3. Select BAKE mode, then set the temperature to 400 F and the time to 25 minutes, then press start.
4. When the display shows Add Food then place the cooking tray in the vortex plus air fryer oven.
5. Serve and enjoy.

Nutritional Value (Amount per Serving):

- Calories 229
- Fat 15 g
- Carbohydrates 1.6 g
- Sugar 0.4 g
- Protein 25.5 g
- Cholesterol 112 mg

Garlicky Mushrooms

Preparation Time: 10 minutes
Cooking Time: 12 minutes
Serve: 2

Ingredients:
- 1 lb mushrooms, clean & stems removed
- 1/8 tsp garlic powder
- 2 tbsp chives, sliced
- 1 tsp garlic, minced
- 1 tbsp olive oil
- 1/8 tsp pepper
- 1/8 tsp kosher salt

Directions:
1. Add mushrooms and remaining ingredients into the large bowl and toss until well coated.
2. Spread mushrooms onto the cooking tray.
3. Select BAKE mode, then set the temperature to 400 F and the time to 12 minutes, then press start.
4. When the display shows Add Food then place the cooking tray in the vortex plus air fryer oven.
5. Serve and enjoy.

Nutritional Value (Amount per Serving):
- Calories 56
- Fat 3.8 g
- Carbohydrates 4.2 g
- Sugar 2 g
- Protein 3.7 g
- Cholesterol 0 mg

Salsa Jalapeno Poppers

Preparation Time: 10 minutes

Cooking Time: 13 minutes

Serve: 2

Ingredients:

- 4 jalapeno peppers, slice in half and deseeded
- 1/4 tsp chili powder
- 1/2 tsp garlic, minced
- 2 tbsp salsa
- 4 oz feta cheese, crumbled
- Pepper
- Salt

Directions:

1. In a small bowl, mix together cheese, salsa, chili powder, garlic, pepper, and salt.
2. Spoon cheese mixture into each jalapeno halves and place onto the cooking tray.
3. Select BAKE mode, then set the temperature to 350 F and the time to 13 minutes, then press start.
4. When the display shows Add Food then place the cooking tray in the vortex plus air fryer oven.
5. Serve and enjoy.

Nutritional Value (Amount per Serving):

- Calories 84
- Fat 6.3 g
- Carbohydrates 2.9 g
- Sugar 1.9 g
- Protein 4.4 g
- Cholesterol 25 mg

Savory Jalapeno Poppers

Preparation Time: 10 minutes

Cooking Time: 10 minutes

Serve: 2

Ingredients:

- 10 jalapenos, cut in half & remove ribs & seeds
- 4 oz cream cheese, softened
- 4 oz cheddar cheese, shredded
- 4 bacon slices, cooked & crumbled
- Pepper
- Salt

Directions:

1. In a bowl, mix together cream cheese, bacon, cheddar cheese, pepper, and salt.
2. Stuff cream cheese mixture into each jalapeno half.
3. Place stuff jalapeno peppers onto the cooking tray.
4. Select BAKE mode, then set the temperature to 350 F and the time to 10 minutes, then press start.
5. When the display shows Add Food then place the cooking tray in the vortex plus air fryer oven.
6. Serve and enjoy.

Nutritional Value (Amount per Serving):

- Calories 218
- Fat 18.3 g
- Carbohydrates 2.3 g
- Sugar 1 g
- Protein 11.1 g
- Cholesterol 55 mg

Tasty Cauliflower Tots

Preparation Time: 10 minutes

Cooking Time: 18 minutes

Serve: 2

Ingredients:

- 1 large egg
- 1 tbsp butter
- 2 cups cauliflower, steamed and shredded
- 1/4 tsp onion powder
- 1/4 tsp garlic powder
- 1/2 cup parmesan cheese, shredded
- Pepper
- Salt

Directions:

1. Add all ingredients into the bowl and mix until well combined.
2. Make small tots from mixture and place onto the cooking tray.
3. Select BAKE mode, then set the temperature to 400 F and the time to 18 minutes, then press start.
4. When the display shows Add Food then place the cooking tray in the vortex plus air fryer oven.
5. Serve and enjoy.

Nutritional Value (Amount per Serving):

- Calories 23
- Fat 1.6 g
- Carbohydrates 0.9 g
- Sugar 0.3 g
- Protein 1.6 g
- Cholesterol 16 mg

Ranch Chicken Wings

Preparation Time: 10 minutes

Cooking Time: 20 minutes

Serve: 2

Ingredients:

- 1 lb chicken wings
- 2 tbsp olive oil
- 1 1/2 tbsp ranch seasoning
- 3 garlic cloves, minced

Directions:

1. Toss chicken wings with garlic, oil, and ranch seasoning.
2. Arrange chicken wings onto the cooking tray.
3. Select AIRFRY mode, then set the temperature to 360 F and the time to 20 minutes, then press start.
4. When the display shows Add Food then place the cooking tray in the vortex plus air fryer oven.
5. Turn chicken wings halfway through.
6. Serve and enjoy.

Nutritional Value (Amount per Serving):

- Calories 290
- Fat 15.4 g
- Carbohydrates 0.7 g
- Sugar 0 g
- Protein 0 g
- Cholesterol 101 mg

Broccoli Cheese Balls

Preparation Time: 10 minutes
Cooking Time: 30 minutes
Serve: 2

Ingredients:

- 2 cups broccoli florets
- 1/4 cup onion, minced
- 1 cup cheddar cheese, shredded
- 1/2 cup almond flour
- 2 eggs, lightly beaten
- 1 tsp Cajun seasoning
- 1 garlic clove, minced
- 2 tbsp fresh cilantro, chopped
- Pepper
- Salt

Directions:

1. Add broccoli into the boiling water and cook until tender.
2. Drain broccoli well and transfer in food processor and process until minced. Transfer to the bowl.
3. Add remaining ingredients and mix until just combined.
4. Make small balls and place them onto the cooking tray.
5. Select BAKE mode, then set the temperature to 400 F and the time to 25-30 minutes, then press start.
6. When the display shows Add Food then place the cooking tray in the vortex plus air fryer oven.
7. Serve and enjoy.

Nutritional Value (Amount per Serving):

- Calories 251
- Fat 18.8 g
- Carbohydrates 8.9 g
- Sugar 2.6 g
- Protein 14.5 g
- Cholesterol 112 mg

Meatballs

Preparation Time: 10 minutes
Cooking Time: 15 minutes
Serve: 2

Ingredients:

- 2 lbs ground turkey
- 1/2 cup coconut flour
- 1 tbsp fresh ginger, grated
- 1 tsp garlic, minced
- 2 tbsp fresh cilantro, chopped
- 2 tbsp green onion, sliced
- 2 eggs, lightly beaten
- 1 tbsp sesame oil
- 1 tsp sea salt

Directions:

1. Add all ingredients into the large bowl and mix until well combined.
2. Make small balls from the meat mixture and place them onto the cooking tray.
3. Select BAKE mode, then set the temperature to 400 F and the time to 15 minutes, then press start.
4. When the display shows Add Food then place the cooking tray in the vortex plus air fryer oven.
5. Serve and enjoy.

Nutritional Value (Amount per Serving):

- Calories 259
- Fat 15.4 g
- Carbohydrates 1.3 g
- Sugar 0.2 g
- Protein 32.7 g
- Cholesterol 157 mg

Chapter 7: Seafood Recipes

Delicious Baked Cod

Preparation Time: 10 minutes
Cooking Time: 25 minutes
Serve: 2

Ingredients:

- 1 lb cod fillets
- 1 1/2 tsp lemon juice
- 1 tsp olive oil
- 1 garlic clove, chopped
- 1/2 tsp pepper
- 1/2 tsp ground cumin
- 1/8 tsp ground turmeric
- 1/2 tsp salt

Directions:

1. Add fish fillets and remaining ingredients into the zip-lock bag, seal bag, and place in the refrigerator overnight.
2. Place marinated fish fillets onto the cooking tray.
3. Select BAKE mode, then set the temperature to 400 F and the time to 20-25 minutes, then press start.
4. When the display shows Add Food then place the cooking tray in the vortex plus air fryer oven.
5. Serve and enjoy.

Nutritional Value (Amount per Serving):

- Calories 105
- Fat 2.3 g
- Carbohydrates 0.6 g
- Sugar 0.1 g
- Protein 20.4 g
- Cholesterol 56 mg

Greek Shrimp

Preparation Time: 10 minutes

Cooking Time: 20 minutes

Serve: 2

Ingredients:

- 1 lb shrimp, peeled and deveined
- 3/4 cup feta cheese, crumbled
- 1/8 tsp red chili flakes
- 1/2 tsp oregano
- 2 garlic cloves, minced
- 1 tbsp olive oil
- 14.5 oz can tomato, diced
- 1/4 tsp salt

Directions:

1. Add shrimp into the baking dish. Mix together remaining ingredients and pour over shrimp.
2. Select BAKE mode, then set the temperature to 375 F and the time to 20 minutes, then press start.
3. When the display shows Add Food then place the baking dish in the vortex plus air fryer oven.
4. Serve and enjoy.

Nutritional Value (Amount per Serving):

- Calories 164
- Fat 11.4 g
- Carbohydrates 8.7 g
- Sugar 4.7 g
- Protein 30.9 g
- Cholesterol 264 mg

Easy Salmon Patties

Preparation Time: 10 minutes

Cooking Time: 7 minutes

Serve: 2

Ingredients:

- 1 egg, lightly beaten
- 8 oz salmon fillet, minced
- 1/4 tsp garlic powder
- Pepper
- Salt

Directions:

1. Add all ingredients into the bowl and mix until well combined.
2. Make small patties from salmon mixture and place onto the parchment-lined cooking tray.
3. Select AIRFRY mode, then set the temperature to 390 F and the time to 7 minutes, then press start.
4. When the display shows Add Food then place the cooking tray in the vortex plus air fryer oven.
5. Serve and enjoy.

Nutritional Value (Amount per Serving):

- Calories 183
- Fat 9.2 g
- Carbohydrates 0.5 g
- Sugar 0.3 g
- Protein 24.8 g
- Cholesterol 132 mg

Chili Prawns

Preparation Time: 10 minutes

Cooking Time: 8 minutes

Serve: 2

Ingredients:

- 6 prawns
- 1 tsp chili flakes
- 1/4 tsp pepper
- 1 tsp chili powder
- 1/4 tsp salt

Directions:

1. In a bowl, add all ingredients and toss well.
2. Transfer prawns onto the cooking tray.
3. Select AIRFRY mode, then set the temperature to 350 F and the time to 6-8 minutes, then press start.
4. When the display shows Add Food then place the cooking tray in the vortex plus air fryer oven.
5. Serve and enjoy.

Nutritional Value (Amount per Serving):

- Calories 83
- Fat 1.4 g
- Carbohydrates 1.9 g
- Sugar 0.1 g
- Protein 15.2 g
- Cholesterol 139 mg

Delicious Baked Tilapia

Preparation Time: 10 minutes
Cooking Time: 15 minutes
Serve: 2

Ingredients:

- 6 tilapia fillets, pat dry with a paper towel
- 1/2 cup Asiago cheese, grated
- 1/4 tsp dried basil
- 1/4 tsp dried thyme
- 1/4 tsp onion powder
- 1/4 tsp garlic powder
- 1/2 cup mayonnaise
- 1/8 tsp black pepper
- 1/4 tsp salt

Directions:

1. Arrange tilapia fillets onto the parchment-lined cooking tray.
2. In a small bowl, mix together mayonnaise, garlic powder, onion powder, thyme, basil, cheese, pepper, and salt.
3. Spread mayonnaise mixture on top of each tilapia fillet.
4. Select BAKE mode, then set the temperature to 350 F and the time to 15 minutes, then press start.
5. When the display shows Add Food then place the cooking tray in the vortex plus air fryer oven.
6. Serve and enjoy.

Nutritional Value (Amount per Serving):

- Calories 125
- Fat 8.9 g
- Carbohydrates 4.9 g
- Sugar 1.3 g
- Protein 6.7 g
- Cholesterol 24 mg

Baked Catfish

Preparation Time: 10 minutes
Cooking Time: 20 minutes
Serve: 2

Ingredients:

- 4 catfish fillets
- 1/4 tsp garlic powder
- 2 tbsp butter, melted
- 1 lemon juice
- 1/2 tsp pepper
- 1/2 tsp dried basil
- 1/2 tsp dried oregano
- 1/2 tsp dried thyme
- 3/4 tsp paprika
- 2 tbsp parsley, chopped
- 1 tsp salt

Directions:

1. Place fish fillets into the baking dish.
2. Mix together the remaining ingredients and pour over fish fillets.
3. Select BAKE mode, then set the temperature to 350 F and the time to 15-20 minutes, then press start.
4. When the display shows Add Food then place the baking dish in the vortex plus air fryer oven.
5. Serve and enjoy.

Nutritional Value (Amount per Serving):

- Calories 274
- Fat 18.1 g
- Carbohydrates 1.1 g
- Sugar 0.4 g
- Protein 25.2 g
- Cholesterol 90 mg

Dill Salmon Patties

Preparation Time: 10 minutes

Cooking Time: 10 minutes

Serve: 2

Ingredients:

- 1 egg
- 14 oz salmon
- 1/4 cup onion, diced
- 1 tsp dill weed
- 1/2 cup almond flour

Directions:

1. Add all ingredients into the bowl and mix well.
2. Make patties from mixture and place onto the parchment-lined cooking tray.
3. Select AIRFRY mode, then set the temperature to 375 F and the time to 10 minutes, then press start.
4. When the display shows Add Food then place the cooking tray in the vortex plus air fryer oven.
5. Serve and enjoy.

Nutritional Value (Amount per Serving):

- Calories 461
- Fat 28.5 g
- Carbohydrates 7.8 g
- Sugar 1.8 g
- Protein 47.5 g
- Cholesterol 169 mg

Chipotle Shrimp

Preparation Time: 10 minutes

Cooking Time: 8 minutes

Serve: 2

Ingredients:

- 1 1/2 lbs shrimp, peeled and deveined
- 2 tsp chipotle in adobo
- 2 tbsp olive oil
- 4 tbsp lime juice
- 1/4 tsp ground cumin

Directions:

1. Add shrimp, oil, lime juice, cumin, and chipotle in a zip-lock bag, seal bag, and place in the fridge for 30 minutes.
2. Thread marinated shrimp onto skewers and place skewers onto the cooking tray.
3. Select AIRFRY mode, then set the temperature to 350 F and the time to 8 minutes, then press start.
4. When the display shows Add Food then place the cooking tray in the vortex plus air fryer oven.
5. Serve and enjoy.

Nutritional Value (Amount per Serving):

- Calories 275
- Fat 10 g
- Carbohydrates 6.4 g
- Sugar 0.7 g
- Protein 39 g
- Cholesterol 359 mg

Shrimp with Cherry Tomatoes

Preparation Time: 10 minutes

Cooking Time: 25 minutes

Serve: 2

Ingredients:

- 1 lb shrimp, peeled and deveined
- 1 tbsp olive oil
- 4 garlic cloves, sliced
- 2 cups grape tomatoes
- 1/2 tsp salt

Directions:

1. Add shrimp and remaining ingredients into the baking dish and mix well.
2. Select BAKE mode, then set the temperature to 400 F and the time to 25 minutes, then press start.
3. When the display shows Add Food then place the baking dish in the vortex plus air fryer oven.
4. Serve and enjoy.

Nutritional Value (Amount per Serving):

- Calories 185
- Fat 5.6 g
- Carbohydrates 6.2 g
- Sugar 2.4 g
- Protein 26.8 g
- Cholesterol 239 mg

Curried Cod Fillets

Preparation Time: 10 minutes
Cooking Time: 10 minutes
Serve: 2

Ingredients:

- 2 cod fillets
- 1/4 tsp curry powder
- 1 tbsp butter, melted
- 1 tbsp basil, sliced
- 1/8 tsp garlic powder
- 1/8 tsp paprika
- 1/8 tsp sea salt

Directions:

1. In a small bowl, mix together curry powder, garlic powder, paprika, and salt and set aside.
2. Place cod fillets onto the cooking tray and brush with butter and sprinkle with dry spice mixture.
3. Select BAKE mode, then set the temperature to 360 F and the time to 10 minutes, then press start.
4. When the display shows Add Food then place the cooking tray in the vortex plus air fryer oven.
5. Garnish with basil and serve.

Nutritional Value (Amount per Serving):

- Calories 143
- Fat 6.8 g
- Carbohydrates 0.4 g
- Sugar 0.1 g
- Protein 20.2 g
- Cholesterol 70 mg

Ginger Garlic Fish Fillet

Preparation Time: 10 minutes
Cooking Time: 20 minutes
Serve: 2

Ingredients:

- 12 oz white fish fillets
- 2 garlic cloves, minced
- 2 tsp ginger, grated
- 1 lime zest
- 2 tbsp butter, cut into pieces
- 1/4 tsp onion powder
- Pepper
- Salt

Directions:

1. Place fish fillets in a baking dish. Top with ginger, garlic, and lime zest.
2. Season with onion powder, pepper, and salt.
3. Spread butter pieces on top of fish fillets.
4. Select BAKE mode, then set the temperature to 350 F and the time to 20 minutes, then press start.
5. When the display shows Add Food then place the baking dish in the vortex plus air fryer oven.
6. Serve and enjoy.

Nutritional Value (Amount per Serving):

- Calories 408
- Fat 24.4 g
- Carbohydrates 3 g
- Sugar 0.3 g
- Protein 42.2 g
- Cholesterol 162 mg

Lemon Garlic Cod

Preparation Time: 10 minutes
Cooking Time: 20 minutes
Serve: 2

Ingredients:

- 1 1/2 lb cod fillet
- 1 lemon, sliced
- 1/4 cup butter, diced
- 4 garlic cloves, minced
- 2 lemon juice
- 2 tbsp olive oil
- Pepper
- Salt

Directions:

1. Place fish fillets in the baking dish and season with pepper and salt.
2. Whisk together garlic, lemon juice, and oil and pour over fish fillets.
3. Arrange butter pieces and lemon slices on top of fish fillets.
4. Select BAKE mode, then set the temperature to 400 F and the time to 20 minutes, then press start.
5. When the display shows Add Food then place the cooking tray in the vortex plus air fryer oven.
6. Serve and enjoy.

Nutritional Value (Amount per Serving):

- Calories 313
- Fat 20.3 g
- Carbohydrates 2.9 g
- Sugar 0.9 g
- Protein 31 g
- Cholesterol 114 mg

Chapter 8: Desserts Recipes

Fudgey Flourless Chocolate Cake

Preparation Time: 10 minutes
Cooking Time: 30 minutes
Serve: 2

Ingredients:

- 3 large eggs
- 1 tbsp vanilla
- 1/2 cup unsweetened cocoa powder
- 3/4 cup coconut sugar
- 1/2 cup butter
- 1 cup unsweetened chocolate chips
- 1/2 tsp sea salt

Directions:

1. Line 8-inch cake pan with parchment paper and set aside.
2. Melt butter in a small saucepan over medium heat then add chocolate chips and remove the pan from heat. Stir until chocolate chips in melted.
3. Add remaining ingredients and whisk until smooth.
4. Pour batter into the prepared cake pan.
5. Select BAKE mode, then set the temperature to 375 F and the time to 30 minutes, then press start.
6. When the display shows Add Food then place the cake pan in the vortex plus air fryer oven.
7. Slice and serve.

Nutritional Value (Amount per Serving):

- Calories 236
- Fat 20.1 g
- Carbohydrates 8.7 g
- Sugar 0.3 g
- Protein 5.1 g
- Cholesterol 67 mg

Coffee Cookies

Preparation Time: 10 minutes

Cooking Time: 15 minutes

Serve: 2

Ingredients:

- 2 eggs, lightly beaten
- 1/4 cup erythritol
- 1/4 cup brewed espresso
- 1 cup almond flour
- 1/2 cup ghee, melted
- 2 tsp baking powder
- 1/2 tbsp cinnamon

Directions:

1. Add all ingredients into the bowl and mix until well combined.
2. Make small cookies from mixture and place onto the parchment-lined cooking tray.
3. Select BAKE mode, then set the temperature to 350 F and the time to 15 minutes, then press start.
4. When the display shows Add Food then place the cooking tray in the vortex plus air fryer oven.
5. Serve and enjoy.

Nutritional Value (Amount per Serving):

- Calories 141
- Fat 13.9 g
- Carbohydrates 6.8 g
- Sugar 0.4 g
- Protein 3 g
- Cholesterol 49 mg

Zesty Lemon Muffins

Preparation Time: 10 minutes

Cooking Time: 15 minutes

Serve: 2

Ingredients:

- 2 eggs, separated
- 1 tsp baking powder
- 1 1/2 cups almond flour
- 1 lemon juice
- 1 lemon zest, grated
- 3 tbsp Swerve
- 1/4 cup heavy cream

Directions:

1. In a mixing bowl, mix together egg yolks, heavy cream, Sweetener, lemon zest, lemon juice, almond flour, and baking powder until well combined.
2. In a separate bowl, beat egg whites until soft peaks form.
3. Slowly add egg whites into the egg yolk mixture and fold well.
4. Divide mixture into the 6 silicone muffin molds.
5. Select BAKE mode, then set the temperature to 350 F and the time to 15 minutes, then press start.
6. When the display shows Add Food then place silicone muffin molds on the cooking tray and place in the vortex plus air fryer oven.
7. Serve and enjoy.

Nutritional Value (Amount per Serving):

- Calories 204
- Fat 17.4 g
- Carbohydrates 7.9 g
- Sugar 1.3 g
- Protein 8 g
- Cholesterol 61 mg

Chocolate Chip Muffins

Preparation Time: 10 minutes

Cooking Time: 12 minutes

Serve: 2

Ingredients:

- 3 eggs
- 1/2 cup unsweetened chocolate chips
- 1 tbsp Swerve
- 1 tsp baking powder
- 1 cup almond flour
- 1 1/2 cups mozzarella cheese, shredded

Directions:

1. In a bowl, whisk eggs with shredded cheese until well combined.
2. Add Swerve, baking powder, and almond flour and mix until well combined.
3. Add chocolate chips and fold well.
4. Divide mixture into the 6 silicone muffin molds.
5. Select BAKE mode, then set the temperature to 400 F and the time to 12 minutes, then press start.
6. When the display shows Add Food then place silicone muffin molds on the cooking tray and place in the vortex plus air fryer oven.
7. Serve and enjoy.

Nutritional Value (Amount per Serving):

- Calories 293
- Fat 23.5 g
- Carbohydrates 10.5 g
- Sugar 0.8 g
- Protein 11.4 g
- Cholesterol 86 mg

Cranberry Bread Loaf

Preparation Time: 10 minutes
Cooking Time: 30 minutes
Serve: 2

Ingredients:

- 1 large egg
- 2 egg whites
- 1/3 cup cassava flour
- 1 tsp vanilla
- 1/2 tbsp vinegar
- 1 tsp stevia
- 3 tbsp cranberries, chopped
- 1/2 tsp baking soda
- 1/2 tbsp cinnamon
- 3 tbsp butter, melted
- 1/4 tsp salt

Directions:

1. In a bowl, whisk egg whites and egg.
2. Add vanilla, vinegar, and butter. Mix well.
3. Add cranberries, salt, stevia, baking soda, cinnamon, and cassava flour. Mix well.
4. Pour batter into the greased loaf pan.
5. Select BAKE mode, then set the temperature to 350 F and the time to 30 minutes, then press start.
6. When the display shows Add Food then place the loaf pan in the vortex plus air fryer oven.
7. Slice and serve.

Nutritional Value (Amount per Serving):

- Calories 48
- Fat 4 g
- Carbohydrates 1.5 g
- Sugar 0.2 g
- Protein 1.4 g
- Cholesterol 28 mg

Banana Almond Butter Bread

Preparation Time: 10 minutes
Cooking Time: 40 minutes
Serve: 2

Ingredients:

- 3 large eggs
- 3 bananas, mashed
- 1/2 tsp baking powder
- 1/4 cup coconut flour
- 1 1/2 tsp vanilla extract
- 1/4 cup coconut oil, melted
- 1/2 cup almond butter
- 1/8 cup chocolate chips
- 1/4 tsp sea salt
- 1/2 tsp cinnamon
- 1/2 tsp baking soda

Directions:

1. In a large bowl, combine together bananas, vanilla, coconut oil, almond butter, and eggs.
2. Add all dry ingredients and mix well to combine.
3. Pour batter into the greased loaf pan.
4. Select BAKE mode, then set the temperature to 350 F and the time to 40 minutes, then press start.
5. When the display shows Add Food then place the loaf pan in the vortex plus air fryer oven.
6. Slice and serve.

Nutritional Value (Amount per Serving):

- Calories 100
- Fat 6.8 g
- Carbohydrates 8.4 g
- Sugar 4.7 g
- Protein 2.2 g
- Cholesterol 47 mg

Zucchini Chocolate Bread

Preparation Time: 10 minutes
Cooking Time: 30 minutes
Serve: 2

Ingredients:

- 2 large eggs
- 1 cup zucchini, shredded
- 1 tbsp cocoa powder
- 1 cup almond butter
- 2 tbsp chocolate chips
- 1/2 tsp baking soda
- 1 tsp apple cider vinegar
- 1 tsp stevia
- 1 tbsp vanilla extract
- 1/4 tsp sea salt

Directions:

1. In a bowl, blend together almond butter, sea salt, cocoa powder, vanilla, stevia, and eggs until 2 minutes.
2. Add vinegar and soda and fold into the batter. Stir in shredded zucchini.
3. Pour batter into the greased loaf pan and then top with chocolate chips.
4. Select BAKE mode, then set the temperature to 350 F and the time to 30 minutes, then press start.
5. When the display shows Add Food then place the loaf pan in the vortex plus air fryer oven.
6. Slice and serve.

Nutritional Value (Amount per Serving):

- Calories 70
- Fat 4.4 g
- Carbohydrates 4.1 g
- Sugar 2.7 g
- Protein 3.3 g
- Cholesterol 63 mg

Healthy Chia Muffins

Preparation Time: 10 minutes

Cooking Time: 35 minutes

Serve: 2

Ingredients:

- 2 tbsp coconut flour
- 20 drops liquid stevia
- 1/4 cup almond flour
- 1/2 cup ground flax
- 2 tbsp ground chia
- 1/4 cup water
- 1/4 tsp vanilla
- 1/4 tsp baking soda
- 1/2 tsp baking powder
- 1 tsp cinnamon

Directions:

1. In a small bowl, add 6 tablespoons of water and ground chia. Mix well and set aside.
2. In a large bowl, mix together ground flax, baking soda, baking powder, cinnamon, coconut flour, and almond flour.
3. Add chia seed mixture, vanilla, water, and stevia and stir to combine.
4. Pour mixture into the 6 silicone muffin molds.
5. Select BAKE mode, then set the temperature to 350 F and the time to 35 minutes, then press start.
6. When the display shows Add Food then place silicone muffin molds on the cooking tray and place in the vortex plus air fryer oven.
7. Serve and enjoy.

Nutritional Value (Amount per Serving):

- Calories 84
- Fat 6 g
- Carbohydrates 6.4 g
- Sugar 0.2 g
- Protein 3.6 g
- Cholesterol 0 mg

Chocolate Macaroon

Preparation Time: 10 minutes
Cooking Time: 20 minutes
Serve: 2

Ingredients:

- 2 eggs
- 1/4 cup coconut oil
- 1/2 tsp baking powder
- 1/4 cup unsweetened cocoa powder
- 3 tbsp coconut flour
- 1 cup almond flour
- 1/3 cup unsweetened coconut, shredded
- 1/3 cup erythritol
- 1 tsp vanilla
- Pinch of salt

Directions:

1. Add all ingredients into the mixing bowl and mix until well combined.
2. Make small balls from mixture and place onto the parchment-lined cooking tray.
3. Select BAKE mode, then set the temperature to 350 F and the time to 15-20 minutes, then press start.
4. When the display shows Add Food then place the cooking tray in the vortex plus air fryer oven.
5. Serve and enjoy.

Nutritional Value (Amount per Serving):

- Calories 79
- Fat 7 g
- Carbohydrates 6 g
- Sugar 0.5 g
- Protein 2.3 g
- Cholesterol 16 mg

Pumpkin Pie

Preparation Time: 10 minutes

Cooking Time: 30 minutes

Serve: 2

Ingredients:
- 3 eggs
- 1/2 cup pumpkin puree
- 1/2 cup cream
- 1/2 cup unsweetened almond milk
- 1/2 tsp cinnamon
- 1 tsp vanilla
- 1/4 cup Swerve

Directions:
1. In a large bowl, add all ingredients and whisk until smooth.
2. Pour pie mixture into the greased baking dish.
3. Select BAKE mode, then set the temperature to 350 F and the time to 30 minutes, then press start.
4. When the display shows Add Food then place the baking dish in the vortex plus air fryer oven.
5. Slice and serve.

Nutritional Value (Amount per Serving):
- Calories 86
- Fat 5.5 g
- Carbohydrates 4.4 g
- Sugar 2 g
- Protein 4.9 g
- Cholesterol 128 mg

Choco Chip Peanut Butter Muffins

Preparation Time: 10 minutes

Cooking Time: 25 minutes

Serve: 2

Ingredients:

- 2 eggs
- 1/3 cup unsweetened coconut milk
- 1/3 cup peanut butter
- 1/3 cup Swerve
- 1 tsp baking powder
- 1/3 cup unsweetened chocolate chips

Directions:

1. In a mixing bowl, mix together all dry ingredients. Add milk and peanut butter and stir to combine.
2. Add eggs and stir until smooth. Add chocolate chips and fold well.
3. Divide mixture into the 8 silicone muffin molds.
4. Select BAKE mode, then set the temperature to 350 F and the time to 25 minutes, then press start.
5. When the display shows Add Food then place silicone muffin molds on the cooking tray and place in the vortex plus air fryer oven.
6. Serve and enjoy.

Nutritional Value (Amount per Serving):

- Calories 169
- Fat 14 g
- Carbohydrates 5 g
- Sugar 1 g
- Protein 5 g
- Cholesterol 41 mg

Pumpkin Butter Cookies

Preparation Time: 10 minutes

Cooking Time: 20 minutes

Serve: 2

Ingredients:

- 1 egg
- 1 tsp vanilla
- 1/2 cup butter
- 1/2 cup pumpkin puree
- 2 cups almond flour
- 1 tsp liquid stevia
- 1/2 tsp pumpkin pie spice

Directions:

1. Add all ingredients into the mixing bowl and mix until well combined.
2. Make small balls from mixture and place onto the parchment-lined cooking tray. Lightly flatten the balls using a fork.
3. Select BAKE mode, then set the temperature to 300 F and the time to 20 minutes, then press start.
4. When the display shows Add Food then place the cooking tray in the vortex plus air fryer oven.
5. Serve and enjoy.

Nutritional Value (Amount per Serving):

- Calories 82
- Fat 7 g
- Carbohydrates 2 g
- Sugar 0.5 g
- Protein 2.1 g
- Cholesterol 15 mg

Chapter 9: Dehydrated Recipes

Simple Tofu Jerky

Preparation Time: 10 minutes
Cooking Time: 4 hours
Serve: 2

Ingredients:

- 1 block tofu, pressed & cut into slices
- 2 tbsp sriracha
- 2 tbsp Worcestershire sauce

Directions:

1. Add tofu slices and remaining ingredients into the zip-lock bag, seal bag, and place in the refrigerator overnight.
2. Arrange tofu slices onto the parchment-lined cooking tray and place the cooking tray in vortex plus air fryer oven.
3. Select DEHYDRATE mode, then set the temperature to 145 F and the time to 4 hours, then press start.
4. Store tofu jerky in an airtight container.

Nutritional Value (Amount per Serving):

- Calories 31
- Fat 1 g
- Carbohydrates 3.4 g
- Sugar 1.6 g
- Protein 1.9 g
- Cholesterol 0 mg

Parmesan Zucchini Chips

Preparation Time: 10 minutes
Cooking Time: 10 hours
Serve: 2

Ingredients:

- 4 cups zucchini slices
- 1 tsp vinegar
- 1/8 tsp garlic powder
- 1 oz parmesan cheese, grated
- 1/8 tsp salt

Directions:

1. Add zucchini slices and remaining ingredients into the mixing bowl and toss well.
2. Arrange zucchini slices onto the cooking tray and place the cooking tray in vortex plus air fryer oven.
3. Select DEHYDRATE mode, then set the temperature to 135 F and the time to 10 hours, then press start.
4. Store zucchini chips in an airtight container.

Nutritional Value (Amount per Serving):

- Calories 41
- Fat 1.7 g
- Carbohydrates 4.1 g
- Sugar 2 g
- Protein 3.7 g
- Cholesterol 5 mg

Delicious BBQ Zucchini Chips

Preparation Time: 10 minutes

Cooking Time: 10 hours

Serve: 2

Ingredients:

- 4 cups zucchini slices
- 3 tbsp BBQ sauce, sugar-free

Directions:

1. Add zucchini slices into the large bowl. Pour BBQ sauce over zucchini slices and toss to coat.
2. Arrange zucchini slices onto the cooking tray and place the cooking tray in vortex plus air fryer oven.
3. Select DEHYDRATE mode, then set the temperature to 135 F and the time to 10 hours, then press start.
4. Store zucchini chips in an airtight container.

Nutritional Value (Amount per Serving):

- Calories 36
- Fat 0.2 g
- Carbohydrates 8 g
- Sugar 5 g
- Protein 1.4 g
- Cholesterol 0 mg

Dehydrated Sweet Peppers

Preparation Time: 10 minutes

Cooking Time: 10 hours

Serve: 2

Ingredients:

- 15 sweet peppers, wash, halve, de-seed & cut into strips

Directions:

1. Arrange sweet peppers onto the cooking tray and place the cooking tray in vortex plus air fryer oven.
2. Select DEHYDRATE mode, then set the temperature to 135 F and the time to 10-12 hours, then press start.
3. Store sweet peppers in an airtight container.

Nutritional Value (Amount per Serving):

- Calories 5
- Fat 0 g
- Carbohydrates 1.1 g
- Sugar 0.8 g
- Protein 0.2 g
- Cholesterol 0 mg

Crisp Green Bean Chips

Preparation Time: 10 minutes

Cooking Time: 8 hours

Serve: 2

Ingredients:

- 2 1/2 lbs green beans, frozen & thawed
- 2 1/2 tbsp coconut oil, melted
- 1/2 tsp garlic powder
- 1/2 tsp onion powder
- 2 tsp salt

Directions:

1. Add green beans into the large bowl. Pour melted oil over green beans and sprinkle with garlic powder, onion powder, and salt and mix well.
2. Arrange green beans onto the cooking tray and place the cooking tray in vortex plus air fryer oven.
3. Select DEHYDRATE mode, then set the temperature to 135 F and the time to 8 hours, then press start.
4. Store green beans in an airtight container.

Nutritional Value (Amount per Serving):

- Calories 105
- Fat 8.5 g
- Carbohydrates 6.3 g
- Sugar 3.1 g
- Protein 1.5 g
- Cholesterol 0 mg

Dehydrated Bell Peppers

Preparation Time: 10 minutes

Cooking Time: 12 hours

Serve: 2

Ingredients:

- 2 green bell peppers
- 1 red bell pepper
- 1 yellow bell pepper

Directions:

1. Cut bell peppers in half, remove seeds & cut into 1/2-inch pieces.
2. Arrange bell pepper pieces onto the parchment-lined cooking tray and place the cooking tray in vortex plus air fryer oven.
3. Select DEHYDRATE mode, then set the temperature to 135 F and the time to 12 hours, then press start.
4. Store bell peppers in an airtight container.

Nutritional Value (Amount per Serving):

- Calories 38
- Fat 0.3 g
- Carbohydrates 9 g
- Sugar 6 g
- Protein 1.2 g
- Cholesterol 0 mg

Healthy Beet Chips

Preparation Time: 10 minutes

Cooking Time: 8 hours

Serve: 2

Ingredients:

- 4 medium beets, peel and sliced
- 1 tbsp salt

Directions:

1. Arrange beet slices onto the cooking tray and sprinkle with salt then place the cooking tray in vortex plus air fryer oven.
2. Select DEHYDRATE mode, then set the temperature to 135 F and the time to 8-10 hours, then press start.
3. Store beet slices in an airtight container.

Nutritional Value (Amount per Serving):

- Calories 44
- Fat 0.2 g
- Carbohydrates 10 g
- Sugar 8 g
- Protein 1.7 g
- Cholesterol 0 mg

Marinated Eggplant Slices

Preparation Time: 10 minutes

Cooking Time: 12 hours

Serve: 2

Ingredients:

- 1 eggplant, sliced
- 1/2 cup vinegar
- 1/2 cup olive oil
- 1 tsp paprika
- 1/2 tsp black pepper
- 1 garlic clove, minced
- 1/2 tsp sea salt

Directions:

1. Add eggplant slices and remaining ingredients into the zip-lock bag, seal bag, and place in the refrigerator for 2 hours.
2. Arrange marinated eggplant slices onto the parchment-lined cooking tray and place the cooking tray in vortex plus air fryer oven.
3. Select DEHYDRATE mode, then set the temperature to 115 F and the time to 12 hours, then press start.
4. Store eggplant slices in an airtight container.

Nutritional Value (Amount per Serving):

- Calories 254
- Fat 25.5 g
- Carbohydrates 7.7 g
- Sugar 3.6 g
- Protein 1.3 g
- Cholesterol 0 mg

Lamb Jerky

Preparation Time: 10 minutes

Cooking Time: 6 hours

Serve: 2

Ingredients:

- 2 lbs boneless lamb, slice into thin strips
- 1 tsp onion powder
- 3 tbsp Worcestershire sauce
- 1/3 cup soy sauce
- 1/2 tsp black pepper
- 1 tbsp oregano
- 1 tsp garlic powder

Directions:

1. Add lamb slices and remaining ingredients into the zip-lock bag, seal bag, and place in the refrigerator overnight.
2. Arrange marinated lamb slices onto the parchment-lined cooking tray and place the cooking tray in vortex plus air fryer oven.
3. Select DEHYDRATE mode, then set the temperature to 145 F and the time to 6 hours, then press start.
4. Store lamb jerky in an airtight container.

Nutritional Value (Amount per Serving):

- Calories 302
- Fat 11.2 g
- Carbohydrates 3.8 g
- Sugar 2 g
- Protein 43.6 g
- Cholesterol 136 mg

Easy Kale Chips

Preparation Time: 10 minutes

Cooking Time: 4 hours

Serve: 2

Ingredients:

- 1 kale heads, clean & cut into pieces
- 1/2 tbsp fresh lemon juice
- 1 1/2 tbsp nutritional yeast
- 1 tbsp olive oil
- 1/2 tsp garlic powder
- 1 tsp sea salt

Directions:

1. Add kale and remaining ingredients into the bowl and mix well.
2. Arrange kale pieces onto the parchment-lined cooking tray and place the cooking tray in vortex plus air fryer oven.
3. Select DEHYDRATE mode, then set the temperature to 145 F and the time to 4 hours, then press start.
4. Store kale chips in an airtight container.

Nutritional Value (Amount per Serving):

- Calories 111
- Fat 7.5 g
- Carbohydrates 8.5 g
- Sugar 0.3 g
- Protein 4.9 g
- Cholesterol 0 mg

Eggplant Chips

Preparation Time: 10 minutes

Cooking Time: 4 hours

Serve: 2

Ingredients:

- 1 eggplant, cut into ¼ inch thick slices
- 1/4 tsp garlic powder
- 1 tsp paprika
- 1/4 tsp onion powder

Directions:

1. Add all ingredients into the bowl and toss well.
2. Arrange eggplant slices onto the parchment-lined cooking tray and place the cooking tray in vortex plus air fryer oven.
3. Select DEHYDRATE mode, then set the temperature to 145 F and the time to 4 hours, then press start.
4. Store eggplant chips in an airtight container.

Nutritional Value (Amount per Serving):

- Calories 31
- Fat 0.3 g
- Carbohydrates 7.3 g
- Sugar 3.6 g
- Protein 1.3 g
- Cholesterol 0 mg

Turkey Jerky

Preparation Time: 10 minutes

Cooking Time: 5 hours

Serve: 2

Ingredients:

- 1 lb turkey meat, cut into thin slices
- 1/3 cup Worcestershire sauce
- 2 tbsp soy sauce
- 2 tsp garlic powder
- 1 tbsp onion powder
- 1 tsp salt

Directions:

1. Add turkey slices and remaining ingredients into the zip-lock bag, seal bag, and place in the refrigerator overnight.
2. Arrange turkey slices onto the parchment-lined cooking tray and place the cooking tray in vortex plus air fryer oven.
3. Select DEHYDRATE mode, then set the temperature to 160 F and the time to 5 hours, then press start.
4. Store turkey jerky in an airtight container.

Nutritional Value (Amount per Serving):

- Calories 228
- Fat 5.7 g
- Carbohydrates 7 g
- Sugar 5.1 g
- Protein 34.1 g
- Cholesterol 86 mg

Conclusion

What if there was a way that you could make easy, affordable, and healthy meat recipes at home in just minutes? The Instant Vortex Air Fryer Oven Cookbook for Two is the answer you've been searching for! This book is different, because each recipe was written to ensure you are able to get the most out of your Instant Vortex Air Fryer Oven. Besides, you'll find all nutritional information and difficult skill for each recipe.

Master the versatile power of your Instant Vortex Air Fryer Oven with this essential cookbook. Make a delicious meal for the whole family in just 30 minutes! Discover how you can transform your Instant Vortex Air Fryer Oven into the centerpiece of your kitchen with this easy-to-follow guide. Now you can save time, money, and start eating healthier versions of your favorite food. Thanks to this revolutionary cookbook!

www.ingramcontent.com/pod-product-compliance
Lightning Source LLC
Chambersburg PA
CBHW081404070526
44583CB00020B/2664